DOUBLE TAP ON LIFE

THE POWER OF BALANCE IN A WORLD THAT CAN'T STOP COMPETING

ARWA BALDIWALA

INDIA • SINGAPORE • MALAYSIA

ISBN
Hardcase 979-8-89699-461-9
Paperback 979-8-89610-353-0

CONTENTS

FOREWORD

Dr. Indu Shahani
President & Chancellor - ATLAS SkillTech University
Former Sheriff of Mumbai

"Every child deserves a champion: a grown-up who believes in them, knows the value of relationships, and pushes them to reach their full potential." Arwa Baldiwala is that champion for a great many. It was evident to me right away when I met her at a career exploration event that she had a unique talent for empowering, inspiring, and nurturing young minds. Her careful preparation and innate rapport with the students developed an atmosphere that fostered growth and self-assurance.

I asked Arwa to become the Academic Director for first-year students at the Indian School of Management Excellence (ISME) because I saw her enthusiasm for teaching and dedication to student growth. She was excellent in this position, turning students into self-assured, self-confident people. Her commitment and influence caused her to take on more duties, such as becoming the Director of School Social Responsibility. In this capacity, she led partnerships with institutions such as Dentsu, Bajaj, and United Way Mumbai, implementing significant projects that enhanced communities and expanded the perspectives of our students.

As Head of School Leadership at the moment, Arwa has revolutionized education by implementing cutting-edge "power skills" courses. Students who complete these programs gain vital skills like resilience, communication, and confidence, all of which are necessary for surviving in the fast-paced, constantly-changing world of today. Her innovative approach equips students for life's unforeseen obstacles as well as for success in the workplace.

Arwa's conviction in the transformational potential of mentoring is what really makes her stand out. She empowers people in addition to teaching. Her impact goes well beyond the classroom; she helps each student she mentors develop resilience and emotional intelligence. She is a prime example of the idea that character development and life shaping are the goals of education.

Arwa's dedication to lifelong learning is admirable. Her desire to stay ahead of the curve and embrace innovation is demonstrated by her pursuit of executive programs at Harvard and IIM Ahmedabad. Her students share this philosophy of constant improvement, emerging as bold, self-aware people equipped to handle the challenges of contemporary life.

Arwa condenses years of experience into useful, doable lessons for today's students, parents, and teachers in her first book, Double Tap on Life. Her conviction that life skills like resilience and confidence are just as important as academic knowledge is reflected in this book. It provides knowledge and tactics to support youth thrive in an increasingly complex and fast-paced world.

Double Tap on Life is more than just a book; it's a manual for educators hoping to develop future leaders, parents looking to connect with their children, and young readers realizing their own potential. It perfectly captures Arwa's mission to develop self-assured, kind people who are capable of leading fulfilling, balanced lives.

It is a privilege for me to endorse the publication of this outstanding book. Numerous lives have been impacted by Arwa's work as a mentor and educator, and this book guarantees that her wisdom will continue to uplift and empower a great number of people."

ADVANCE PRAISE

D. Sivanandhan, IPS,
Former DGP of Maharashtra State

"*Double Tap on Life* is a voice of clarity in today's overwhelming world. Through profound insights and her personal and very relatable stories, Arwa Baldiwala challenges readers to reflect deeply, act courageously, and embrace their true potential. The chapter on 'The 3 H's – Head, Heart, and Hand' is a masterful synthesis of intellect, compassion, and purposeful action, offering a timeless approach to living a balanced and meaningful life. This book is more than a read, it's an invitation to rediscover your strength, reimagine your priorities, and transform your everyday choices into lasting impact. For anyone seeking inspiration, *Double Tap on Life* is a truly remarkable guide to living with intention and integrity."

Sandip Soparrkar
Bollywood Choreographer, Actor, Columnist

"I have had the privilege of knowing Arwa Baldiwala as a visionary educator and youth mentor for over a decade, and I have been fortunate to have her as my dance student as well. Her dedication to impactful education, coupled with her transformative leadership, extends far beyond academics, earning her immense respect from everyone she inspires, including me. As a debut author, her book *Double Tap on Life* is a reflection of her brilliance and unwavering commitment to empowerment. Among its many gems, the chapter 'Mental Gym' stands out as a powerful exploration of mental health, offering practical and transformative insights. The timeless Shloka, *Asatoma Sadgamaya, Tamasoma Jyotir Gamaya, Mrityorma Amritam Gamaya,* resonates deeply with her vision, leading us from illusion to truth, darkness to light, and, through this book, from mortality to immortality. Truly inspiring, this is a must-read for anyone seeking purpose and growth."

Rishabh Shah
Founder, Indias International Movement to Unite Nations

"I have always believed that 'adversity is the mother of all opportunity.' I have known her during her time as Head of School and during that time she has led a principled life converting every adversity into opportunity. Using her life journey as the canvas, this self-help book is a useful tool for anyone who is looking at learning how to optimise themselves."

Dr. Kersi Chavda
Consultant Psychiatrist
Past President, Bombay Psychiatric Society

"Arwa has spent over 22 years in the education sector and has won several accolades in her field. I have the privilege of writing a foreword for her book, *Double Tap on Life*, based on the experiences she has had through her remarkable career.

Within these pages lies not a prescription, but a guide. It is not meant to tell you who you should be, but to assist you in discovering who you already are. Here, you will find tools to strengthen your character, insights to illuminate your path, and wisdom to inspire action toward the life you've always envisioned.

Becoming the best version of yourself is not about perfection—it's about progress. It's about leaning into the challenges, embracing the unknown, and fostering a mindset that turns obstacles into opportunities. This is not a one-size-fits-all roadmap; it is a mirror reflecting back the infinite possibilities that exist within you.

We all need to remember this: greatness is not a gift reserved for the few. It is a practice available to all. It begins with intention, grows through persistence, and thrives when you choose to rise again and again, in spite of the millions of obstacles that come in your path.

This book is your invitation, to reflect, to evolve, and to thrive. Let it meet you where you are and guide you to where you are meant to be. The journey begins now, and it belongs to you."

PREFACE

Double Tap on Life began as a simple idea: to share the lessons learned from life's inevitable ups and downs, and to offer a roadmap for anyone looking to own their journey with greater resilience and authenticity. In an era where we are constantly bombarded with images of perfection and success, it's easy to lose sight of what truly matters. This book is my attempt to peel back the layers of that illusion and to explore what it really means to live fully, even in the face of adversity.

Writing this book was a deeply personal journey, one that forced me to confront my own fears, doubts, and challenges. But it was also a journey of healing and empowerment. My hope is that through these pages, you'll find not only the comfort of shared experiences but also the tools and insights you need to cultivate your own mental and emotional wellbeing. This book is for anyone who has ever felt overwhelmed by the pressures of life, who has struggled with loss or self-doubt, and who is ready to start tapping into their own strength and potential.

Thank you for choosing to embark on this journey with me. I promise that what lies ahead is more than just a story—it's an invitation to transform your life, one page, one feeling, one moment at a time.

THANK YOU, FROM THE HEART

No book is ever the result of a single effort. As I bring *Double Tap on Life* to life, I am deeply grateful for the individuals who have supported and inspired me along the way.

To my daughter, Zahra Baldiwala—your creative spirit and endless curiosity fill my life with joy. Our conversations about the stars, the universe and everything in between remind me to dream big and find magic in the ordinary. You are my muse, and I'm forever inspired by you.

To my son, Zaheer Baldiwala—my steadfast anchor and constant cheerleader. Your words, "Mom, just start—one page, one feeling at a time," pushed me through doubt. Your belief in me is a gift I cherish every day.

To my mother, Zainab Bootwala, whose calm serenity and quiet strength have been my unwavering foundation through every high and low And to my brother, Mustafa Bootwala—always just one call away, whose proud words, *"Bravo, Arwa,"* have been my greatest encouragement. Your love and belief light my path.

To Dr. Indu Shahani and Farzana Dohadwala—visionary educationists whose wisdom has shaped my journey. As your protégé, I've grown at every step. Thank you for being such pivotal figures in my life

To Dean Katherine K. Merseth of the Harvard Graduate School of Education—your words, *"Arwa, make no mistake, you are headed for greater places,"* gave me the confidence to pursue this dream. Thank you for believing in my potential.

To my editor, Abhigyan Chakravorty—my Bengali babu, whose patience and understanding have been instrumental in shaping this book. Your support has been truly invaluable.

To Tasneem Rajkotwala—your beautiful illustrations have brought each chapter to life, adding a magical touch to this book. Thank you for your brilliance.

To my students, who connect with me in this digital age—this book is for you. *Double Tap on Life* is a testament to your resilience and the bond we share. Your strength inspires me.

To my readers and critics—I am not perfect, and I welcome your perspectives. If I've ever fallen short, please accept my apologies, as honesty has been my intent. I promise to keep improving.

And finally, thank you, Almighty, for Your countless blessings and for guiding me to this page.

Chapter 1

UNVEILING THE LAYERS WITHIN

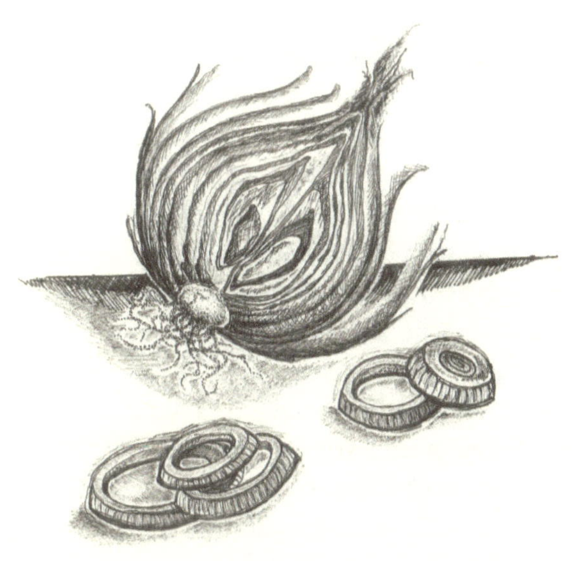

Have you ever asked yourself, "Who am I, really?" while you gazed into the mirror? And no, I'm not talking about bad hair days. We all struggle with this query sometimes. It's an intriguing and intimidating question at the same time. The good news is that you already possess the solution. We're going to explore your values and passions, the cornerstones of a meaningful existence. Let me tell you about two of my former students who were dealing with this dilemma on a daily basis.

Priya always felt alive when she was on stage, basking in the spotlight and delivering powerful performances that left the audience mesmerised. Ever since she was a kid, she was a social butterfly who thrived on stage. She excelled in debate competitions and legal studies, impressing her teachers and peers with her sharp intellect and persuasive arguments. Her parents recognised these abilities but expected her to pursue a more conventional and academically-oriented path, overlooking her true passion for the performing arts. Despite their well-intentioned advice, Priya couldn't shake the passion burning within her for the stage. Can you imagine the frustration?

Rohan, on the other hand, was a natural tinkerer. He could take apart and rebuild almost anything, and his mind buzzed with ideas for inventions. But traditional classroom learning often felt stifling to him. He struggled to sit still for long periods, and his creative energy was shunned by rote memorisation and standardised tests. Rohan wasn't lazy or unintelligent; he simply learned best by doing. He felt like a square peg trying to fit into a round hole.

Priya and Rohan's stories illustrate the power of self-discovery. It wasn't until she stumbled upon a local theatre production that Priya's true calling became clear. Watching the actors breathe life into their characters and transport the audience to different worlds ignited a fire within her that she couldn't ignore. It was as if a veil had been lifted, revealing the path she was meant to tread. Today, Priya is a rising star in the theatre world, captivating audiences with her raw talent and magnetic presence. She has appeared in acclaimed productions and carved out a niche for herself; and guess what, her parents are happy too!

Rohan's journey was a little different. He discovered that his passion for tinkering was a reflection of his core strength – innovation. He decided to explore his options beyond traditional college and enrolled in a vocational programme that focused on machining and product design. This hands-on learning environment was a perfect fit for Rohan. He thrived, his creativity blossoming under the guidance of experienced instructors. Today, Rohan is a product designer at a cutting-edge robotics company, developing innovative solutions that are making a real impact in the world. His days are filled with challenges and opportunities to learn and grow, all while using his skills to create something new and exciting.

Their stories truly highlight the fact that values and passions are great motivators in leading a life that's quite fruitful. If your life's a play, then your core tenets, those values and passions that you hold close to your heart, are the directors of the play; and you can only be successful when you listen to them intently. Of course, life will never ever go as per your plans, but having a compass in your back pocket always helps. Sometimes, the blockbuster play that is life passes you by in a wink, so why not give it an Oscar-worthy performance.

And hey, there are no rules to this; values and passions are just like fashion trends; some come and go, and others become your staples. As you develop and gain new knowledge, they may change partially, or sometimes even completely; and that's totally fine. Today, you may be into poetry, consuming Hemingway like popcorn; yesterday, you might've wanted to pursue badminton full-time. That's completely fine! The key is to remain loyal to who you are and who you are becoming. Stay open to the idea of self-discovery. Now that you know this, it might be a good time to get started on exploring how we can discover your values and passions that are all dying to emerge from obscurity, all while walking the fine line between finding your truest self and circumventing the curveballs that life throws at you.

Values: What Are They?

Values are the cornerstone of your personality, as we've established, but what does it really mean? These are the guiding ideas and precepts that determine your choices, direct your behaviour, and eventually form the essence of who you are.

The wonderful thing about values is that they aren't these inflexible, universal declarations. They are a kaleidoscope of beliefs that mirror your experiences, character, and goals; they are as distinct and colourful as a fingerprint. While honesty may be the cornerstone of every encounter for one individual, adventure and the excitement of the unknown may be prioritised by another.

There is no right or incorrect answer; what matters is what genuinely speaks to you.

Let's explore some fundamental qualities of values:

Core Beliefs: Values are strongly held beliefs that guide your long-term actions and decisions. They are definitely not fleeting and slowly start to become a large part of your moral compass. When you are confused about something, upon introspection, more often than not, you'll find yourself taking guidance from your core values.

Motivational Force: They're your #Everyday Motivation. This means that you get immense joy every time you make a decision that's in line with your values; kind of like those really satisfying slime videos online.

Decision-Making Filter: To be able to fully enjoy the perfect cup of chai, you'll have to strain out the bitter tea leaves first. Your values are that strainer, and the chai is the decision you made that you're happy with. You make most decisions by weighing them against your values.

Evolving Compass: Imagine if the maps app on your phone started showing you maps from ten years ago. That would be so absurd! Values are similar; they aren't set in stone. As you gain more experiences from life, learn new things, and encounter perspectives that are very different from your own, your values may evolve and adapt too. That's perfectly natural, and you need to allow it.

What Values Aren't

Sometimes, you might confuse knock-offs for the real deal. Here they are:

Social Pressures: A lot of times, we are consciously and subconsciously influenced by society about what we should value, what we should wear, what degree we should hold, and what social standing we should have. Even though they might attract you at first (like those super-trendy but super-tiny handbags that are going viral, which I just don't get), they may not be genuine to you. You need to put your foot down and truly resist the urges of letting others change your mind.

Fleeting Desires: You know that feeling when you watch a new show or movie and totally fall in love with a character, and all you can do is try to emulate how amazing they are the following week? I've been there too, but that's all for fun. You can't possibly let a fleeting desire to be something you're not derail your actual values. Fleeting desires are totally fine if we know what we're dealing with. But we should never confuse them for core principles.

Conditional Beliefs: True values are conditional; and they remain true regardless of the circumstance. For example, if you only adhere to honesty when it's convenient to you, it cannot be a value. If it truly is a value, you will let it guide you throughout all circumstances.

The Complexities of Values: Investigating Grey Areas

Figuring out your values will never be black and white; it may sound easy to say that you value something, but in practice, over time, you'll find many loopholes in your value system.

"Clarifying one's values and investing in activities aligned with those values can lead to greater life satisfaction and fulfilment. For example, identifying valued life domains and setting goals based on those domains can enhance overall wellbeing."

Source: https://positivepsychology.com/good-life/, Jo Nash, Ph.D.

Here's what you can do to try to tackle those grey areas:

Open Communication: Sometimes, an honest and open discussion can be very helpful in resolving a conflict of values. If you find yourself in a situation where your values seem to contradict someone else's, have a calm and respectful conversation. Explain your perspective and try to understand theirs. You might be surprised to find common ground or even discover a creative solution that honours both sets of values.

Seek Perspective: Remember this, whatever the predicament, speaking with a trusted friend, mentor, or therapist will always help you clear your head. Their unbiased and external viewpoint can help you look at a problem through a fresh lens and might eventually help you determine which values matter the most to you.

Growth Mindset: I might sound like a broken record, but I'll say it again. Figuring out your values will always be a lifelong process. There's no formula to it. You will make errors or decide on a course of action that isn't entirely consistent with the values you uphold; it happens to the best of us. The true lesson in this is to take what you can from them and turn them into chances for personal growth. So don't set yourself up for failure; just trust the process.

Back in 2019, I came across a beautiful story that has really stayed with me. I'm always looking for a new hobby, and that year, it was pottery. I met Agnes at the pottery studio; and even though that hobby never really picked up, I definitely picked up a lesson for the ages:

you can discover your passion at any age. Agnes was a banker all her life; a career woman through and through, so I automatically assumed that she'd have a rock-solid understanding of who she was and her priorities. However, Agnes experienced a sense of misalignment following retirement.

"I spent so much time climbing the corporate ladder that I forgot to ask myself why I was climbing it in the first place."

Agnes acknowledged that for her, responsibility came before purpose. Seeing someone at her age so receptive to self-exploration was very encouraging. Initially, she thought of pottery as just another pastime, but something started to change as Agnes sculpted the cool, damp clay. The same hands that used to handle financial documents all day found a new meaning in shaping bowls and mugs. Agnes realised her true value – creation. In this quiet haven away from the responsibilities of daily life, she did more than just create beautiful ceramics; she gave expression to her creativity and rekindled a long-dormant aspect of herself back to life.

What are Passions?

We have talked about the concept of values, but there is another part of the self-discovery puzzle: passions. Think about your passion as a fire that starts from a spark and ignites you, activities or interests that give you great pleasure and satisfaction. They are things that make us forget ourselves in time, activities that leave us feeling active and truly alive.

Contrary to hobbies, which may come and go, passions are deeply ingrained within you. They appeal to your innermost yearnings, making life meaningful beyond just the daily grind. For some, it might be the thrill of creating music, the satisfaction of helping others, or the intellectual challenge of solving complex problems. Your passions have the potential to change your life.

Here's how you can recognise your passions:

Passion is the Reward: When you're truly immersed in your passion, you don't need any external validation or reward for it. The passion is the incentive, and your desire for it will always satisfy you.

Energy Boosters: Engaging in your passions has a revitalising effect. It can leave you feeling energised, inspired, and ready to tackle the world. They are your personal wellspring of motivation and creativity.

Flow State: Have you ever sat down to create art or read a book, only to realise by the end of it how time seemed to melt away? That's you in a 'flow state', in which you're completely absorbed in the task and all your surroundings no longer matter.

Lifers: I like to call my passions, lifers. While you may not turn to your passions with the same kind of intensity all the time, that doesn't mean that they're not always there for you. Like values, they too can evolve and adapt, but the core essence remains the same.

That's Not a Passion!

We've seen how to spot a real value from a dupe; now let's see what passions are definitely not:

External Validation: Passions are not a game of likes and shares. External validation should be like water off a duck's back if your passion is authentic. True passions are driven by an internal desire for growth and fulfilment, not external recognition.

Passing Trends: The latest fad or trendy activity might pique your interest for a short while, but it's not a passion if it doesn't ignite a spark within you. Passions are enduring sources of joy and motivation, not fleeting fancies.

Obligations: Don't mistake obligations or commitments for passions. While you might find some aspects of a certain activity enjoyable, it's not a passion if you don't feel a deep sense of fulfilment from engaging in it.

Turn that Spark into a Fire

Now that you are aware of the influence of passions, how can you use them to create a fulfilling life? Here are some pointers:

Accept Exploration: Don't ever be scared to explore new things and venture beyond your comfort zone. You never know what hidden passions are in store for you. As an English teacher, I had zero clue that I would even be teaching business communication classes someday.

Make Time: I think maturing is realising that all good things take time. So, when you are trying to positively channelise your passions, it is extremely important to allocate a specific period of time each day or week to pursuing your interests. Give it the same consideration as you would any other important obligation.

Find Your Tribe: I've lost count of the number of times I have been completely taken aback by great insights and encouragement that I receive on the daily from my connections. The *World Values Survey* found that across the globe, family, work, and friends are consistently ranked as the most important aspects of life. Over 90% of respondents in nearly all countries ranked family as "very important." For you to realise the full potential of your values and passions, you have to find others who are cut from the same cloth as you. That's a non-negotiable.

Start Small: You don't have to turn your daily tasks upside down; you can just start by including tiny elements of your passions into your daily routine.

Self-Discovery Driven by Passions and Values

The process of self-discovery can be thrilling and uncertain at the same time; quite like a treasure hunt. With a fresh understanding of your passions and values, you have just what you need to explore further. If you imagine your life as a treasure hunt, the treasure you seek is that profound sense of contentment and direction.

Your values serve as a compass, pointing you in the direction of opportunities, actions, and decisions that are fundamentally consistent with your identity. Your inner flame is stoked by your passions, which are what motivate and excite you to move forward. You'll travel through many different terrains on this journey of self-discovery, including clear, straight highways, winding alleys, and even impenetrable woods of self-doubt. But now, you know who you are and what you want, which is a great starting point for navigating these challenges.

This treasure hunt will push you to excavate layers of sediment to uncover hidden artefacts. You'll have to peel back the layers of conditioning, societal expectations, and past experiences to reveal the essence of who you truly are. Once you introspect, you'll have clear answers to questions like, 'What patterns, beliefs, and behaviours have shaped your identity?' and 'Are there any aspects in your life that you've outgrown?'.

The world we live in constantly encourages conformity, and sometimes, the drive to be authentic can be misconstrued as a radical act of rebellion, even to yourself. Once you learn to unsee this conformist societal view and start embracing those quirks that make you so beautifully human, you'll be on your way to leading a life that makes you happy, and your values and passions can act as the guideposts on your journey.

Navigating the Rapids

On your way to self-discovery, you will come across many unexpected roadblocks. Nevertheless, there are watershed moments in the midst of these struggles. At the early stages of my journey of self-actualisation, it was critical when my brother suggested that I join Orchid as a finishing school. Through this programme, I got an extraordinary chance to develop my talents in a conducive environment.

Under the direction of the renowned producer and actress Anuradha Patel, Orchid provided a safe haven for people like me to thrive. But even with the priceless teachings and opportunities Orchid presented, I ran against roadblocks and difficulties that could have easily derailed my progress. I especially struggled in the sphere of public speaking and networking.

It was during these times that my brother really came through as a strong support system. He truly believed that Orchid could prove to be extremely beneficial for my personal and professional development. Despite having plenty of his own commitments, he went above and beyond to ensure that I would attend the sessions, often waiting until late in the evenings to ensure that I didn't have to go back home alone.

That phase of my life has always been a constant reminder to me that you don't have to navigate the rapids alone and that it's okay to ask for help. I'll say it before you realise it the hard way – you have to accept the support of your mentors and loved ones because, believe it or not, sometimes they see potential in you that you may not see yourself. Their wisdom and encouragement can be just what you need to handle problems with resilience and grace.

Key Learnings

1. Values are your guideposts; they encapsulate everything from shaping your decisions to providing clarity and purpose in your life.
2. If you're laser-focused and probably also smiling ear-to-ear while doing a task, chances are, that's a passion. They are deeply rooted sources of joy that align us with our most authentic selves.
3. Battles are never fought alone, and self-discovery is just as good as a modern-day battle. A little support and encouragement from your loved ones and mentors can go a long way.

Action Items

1. The best way to get acquainted with your values and passions is through thorough introspection. Sometimes, jotting down the principles that guide most of your decisions is a great way to understand who you really are.
2. Don't let fear or uncertainty hold you back from pursuing your dreams. Take concrete steps towards aligning your life with your values and passions. Whether it's enrolling in a course, joining a club, or simply dedicating more time to activities you love, make a commitment to yourself to take action.
3. Reach out to friends, family members, or mentors who can offer support and guidance on your journey of self-discovery. Share your goals and aspirations with them and ask for their input and encouragement. Consider seeking out a professional coach or therapist for additional support and accountability.

Chapter 2

DONE DOUBTING

Now, you know your values and passions, but have you accepted them? In this chapter, we'll be going further into the meaning of self-confidence and find out how to develop this crucial trait. Self-confidence is quite a loosely used term these days. Having the best style, or coming up with witty remarks in social situations doesn't make up what it truly means to be confident in yourself.

Choosing to Accept Oneself

Accepting yourself is the first step on the path to self-confidence. I think this will be best conveyed through a story from my life.

Growing up in a conservative home, I constantly felt like I was being watched. Every action and every word I spoke, and even the way I walked and dressed, were constantly under the radar. From the clothes I wore to the way I styled my hair, the list just went on and on. There were some pretty strong expectations that were dictating how I presented myself to the world. But my appearance was just the tip of the iceberg; my aspirations were also kept in check. The idea of pursuing higher education was met with intense scepticism, and at the end of the day, I was always pigeonholed into believing that my purpose in life was to find a suitable match and settle down with kids. This situation made me question myself; I was so busy trying to appease everyone that I completely lost myself in the process. I didn't know what I wanted from life. I was constantly being pulled in two directions, one urging me to comply with societal expectations and the other pushing me to follow my dreams. In this environment, seeking validation became second nature to me. I craved approval from everyone around me – my family, my peers, even strangers on the street. I believed that if I could just meet their standards of acceptability, I would be worthy.

It wasn't until much later, after years of feeling trapped in this cycle of seeking external validation, that I finally began my journey of self-discovery. I began to question the narrative that had been imposed upon me and started to explore my own interests and passions. Through education, both formal and informal, I gained knowledge and perspective that helped me break free from the constraints of my upbringing. I pursued courses at prestigious universities, expanding my horizons and challenging myself in ways I had never imagined possible.

But embracing self-acceptance isn't a cakewalk. The only way to truly accept yourself is through vulnerability, courage, and a willingness to confront our deepest insecurities. Of course, like any process that involves introspection, this too will come with its own set of triumphs and setbacks. Yet, it is through this journey that we lay the foundation for genuine self-confidence - a confidence that stems from an unwavering belief in our inherent worthiness, regardless of external circumstances.

Today, I've truly come to appreciate the importance of self-acceptance. You have to break some glass ceilings on your way to embracing who you truly are, and you have to do it unapologetically. My life has been fraught with challenges that have made me question my worth, but that doesn't have to be the way for others. Which is why the earlier you learn to accept yourself, the faster you'll unlock your full and true potential.

Cultivating Growth Mindset

Having a growth mindset is essential to realise our full potential in a world that is continuously changing and expanding. However, what is a growth mindset exactly, and how can we foster one in our own lives? In the early years of my teaching profession, my life was constantly riddled with nerves and anxiety. Sometimes, even something as fundamental as stepping into the classroom to deliver a complex lesson or speaking in front of my colleagues at a staff meeting shook my confidence, clouding it with the dread of failure.

I can still clearly recall the times when I would feel like I was about to have a panic attack because I was so full of confusion and self-doubt. I would feverishly contact my mom in times of such despair, hoping that she'd have a solution to this gargantuan problem.

The idea of a growth mindset came to me like a knight in shining armour when I was wallowing in self-doubt. My life was drastically altered by the realisation that intelligence and ability are not set in stone; they can be easily developed and improved with effort and perseverance. Armed with this newfound perspective, I made a conscious effort to confront my fears head-on and embrace challenges as opportunities for growth. Instead of avoiding situations that triggered my anxiety, I challenged myself to step outside of my comfort zone and take calculated risks, knowing that even failure held valuable lessons to be learned.

Slowly but surely, I began to see progress. What once seemed like insurmountable obstacles became manageable hurdles, and the crippling fear that once held me back began to lose its grip on my psyche. I transitioned from a person who relied on memorised scripts and cue cards to deliver a speech to someone who could confidently speak off the cuff, trusting in my ability to communicate effectively and authentically. It's easier than you think. These are the steps I followed:

1. Practice in a Supportive Environment: I'd be at the dinner table, fork in one hand, speech notes in the other, delivering my lines to an audience of supportive family members. Their nods of encouragement and occasional applause made me feel like I was already on stage. Starting in such a cosy, familiar setting helped ease my nerves and build my confidence step by step.

2. Record and Review: I recorded myself giving speeches, presentations, and even just casual chats. Watching the playback was like holding up a mirror to my performance. I cringed at first, noticing every stumble and hesitation, but each review was a chance to learn and improve. It was like having a personal coach – albeit a slightly awkward one!

3. Utilise Visual Aids: Standing in front of the mirror, I transformed into my own audience. I watched as my reflection mimicked every gesture and expression, from animated hand movements to subtle facial cues. It felt a bit silly at first, but over time, I began to see a confident, assured speaker staring back at me.

4. Incorporate Storytelling: As I delved deeper into the world of public speaking, I discovered the magic of storytelling. I realised that it wasn't just about delivering facts and figures; it was about weaving a narrative that resonated with my audience. So, I dug

into my own experiences, sharing anecdotes and insights that added depth and authenticity to my speeches. Each story became a thread connecting me to my listeners, bridging the gap between speaker and audience in a way that no rehearsed speech ever could.

A growth mindset is rooted in the belief that our abilities and intelligence can be developed through dedication, effort, and perseverance. It's about viewing challenges as opportunities for learning and growth, rather than insurmountable obstacles. When we adopt a growth mindset, we embrace the process of learning and development, recognising that success is not determined by innate talent, but rather by our willingness to put in the work and persist in the face of adversity.

But cultivating a growth mindset requires intentionality and practice. It's about reframing our thoughts and beliefs, challenging our fixed notions of success and failure, and embracing the journey of continuous improvement. By adopting a growth mindset, we empower ourselves to overcome obstacles, seize opportunities, and unlock our full potential.

Embrace challenges, learn from failure, and cultivate a mindset of resilience and perseverance. For it is through this that we can truly harness the power of self-confidence and achieve greatness in all areas of our lives.

Harnessing the Power of Positive Self-Talk
Our inner dialogue shapes our reality more than we realise. But how often do we stop to consider the impact of our self-talk on our self-confidence and overall wellbeing?

Positive self-talk is rooted in the belief that we are worthy, capable, and deserving of success and happiness. It's about reframing negative thoughts and beliefs into positive affirmations that empower and uplift us. When we practice positive self-talk, we cultivate a mindset of self-compassion and resilience, allowing us to surpass life's challenges with grace and confidence. But harnessing the power of positive self-talk requires mindfulness and intentionality; becoming aware of our inner dialogue and actively replacing negative thoughts with positive affirmations. Research from *Mindfulness Meditation: A Pathway to Reducing Fear*, conducted by Harvard Medical School in 2022, shows that mindfulness meditation can reduce the size of the amygdala, the brain region associated with fear, after just 8 weeks of practice. This physical change correlates with reduced stress and anxiety levels. So whether it is through daily meditation, journaling, or affirmations, incorporating positive self-talk into our daily routine can have a profound impact on our self-esteem and mental health.

I challenge you to become more mindful of your inner dialogue and practice positive self-talk in your own life. Embrace words of encouragement, affirm your worthiness, and cultivate a mindset of self-love and empowerment.

Setting Realistic Goals

Goals are the roadmap to our dreams, guiding us towards success and accomplishment. But how do we set goals that are both inspiring and attainable? You must not set ambitious goals for yourself without considering the feasibility or practicality of achieving them. Many times in my life, I was driven by a desire to prove myself and achieve success at all costs, regardless of the toll it took on my wellbeing. As a result, I found myself overwhelmed, burnt out, and disillusioned with my pursuit of success; I see this happening a lot, especially with the youth who are constantly hyper-stimulated by so many aspects of life and the different pressures that come with growing up in the digital age.

It wasn't until I learned to set realistic goals that I began to experience a sense of clarity, purpose, and satisfaction in my life. Realistic goals are those that align with our values, priorities, and capabilities, taking into account our strengths, limitations, and resources. When we set realistic goals, we set ourselves up for success by creating a clear roadmap that guides our actions and decisions. But setting realistic goals isn't just about avoiding disappointment or failure; it's about fostering a sense of self-efficacy and empowerment. When we achieve realistic goals, we build confidence in our ability to set, pursue, and achieve our aspirations, fuelling a cycle of motivation and success.

You must reflect on your own goals. Are they realistic and attainable, or are they based on unrealistic expectations or external pressures? By setting realistic goals that align with your values and capabilities, you can chart a course towards success and fulfilment with confidence and clarity. Here's how you can set realistic and attainable goals for yourself:

1. Reflect on Your Values and Priorities: Take time to align your goals with your core values and aspirations.

This ensures that your objectives are meaningful and fulfilling.

2. Set Specific, Measurable Goals: Clearly define what you want to achieve and establish measurable milestones to track your progress. This specificity provides clarity and focus, making it easier to create actionable plans.

3. Consider Resources and Timeframes: Assess the resources available to you and set realistic timeframes for achieving your goals. Recognise any constraints or limitations and adjust your expectations accordingly.

4. Create Actionable Steps and Stay Flexible: Break down your goals into actionable steps and adapt your plans as needed. Stay flexible and open to adjustments based on feedback and changing circumstances. This approach ensures progress while allowing for necessary modifications along the way.

5. Seek Support and Accountability: Share your goals with trusted friends, family members, or mentors who can offer support and encouragement along the way. Consider joining a support group or finding an accountability partner to help you stay motivated and accountable for your progress. Additionally, seeking guidance from a professional career or life coach can provide valuable insights and personalised strategies to help you overcome challenges and achieve your goals more effectively.

By following these actionable steps, you can set realistic goals that are aligned with your values and aspirations.

Confronting Our Fears

Fear is the shadow that lurks in the corners of our minds, holding us back from reaching our full potential. But what if we could confront our fears head-on and emerge stronger on the other side? Let me share with you a personal story that illustrates the transformative power of facing our fears.

During my time teaching at the Indian School of Management and Entrepreneurship (ISME) in Lower Parel, I was tasked with hosting an orientation session for incoming first-year students and their parents. Confident in my abilities, having conducted similar presentations numerous times before, I stepped onto the stage prepared to deliver a seamless presentation to the audience of over 800 individuals.

However, after a perfect first twenty minutes, I suddenly found myself blanking out. The once-familiar auditorium felt disorienting, and the eyes of the Dean, Vice Dean, and principals of the top institutions in Mumbai bore down on me. Despite my best efforts, panic set in, and I struggled to find my words. Sweating profusely, goosebumps prickling my skin, and my mouth dry, I faltered under the pressure.

In that moment of vulnerability, I made a decision to pivot. Cutting the presentation short, I opened the floor to discussion, allowing the audience to engage and share their thoughts. Though I longed to retreat and hide my embarrassment back then, in retrospect, I recognised the valuable lesson hidden within the experience. This incident taught me the importance of preparation beyond rote learning and the fallibility of relying solely on familiarity. Confronting my fear of failure head-on, I emerged from that challenging moment with a newfound understanding of resilience and adaptability.

According to *Exposure Therapy for Anxiety*, published by the American Psychological Association in 2020, exposure therapy, which involves facing fears in a controlled environment, has a 60% to 90% success rate in treating anxiety disorders, including phobias and Post-Traumatic Stress Disorder (PTSD). Now that doesn't mean that you must force yourself into every situation that induces fear, but you can definitely take control of your fears by following these simple steps:

1. Identify and Understand Your Fears: Start by clearly identifying your fears and understanding what triggers them. Reflect on the situations or experiences that make you feel anxious or scared, and delve deeper into the root cause of these fears.

2. Challenge Negative Thoughts: Fear often stems from negative thoughts and beliefs. Challenge these thoughts by questioning their rationality and replacing them with more balanced perspectives. Avoid catastrophising or jumping to conclusions, and focus on realistic assessments of the situation.

3. Take Gradual Steps: Confronting fears doesn't mean diving headfirst into the deep end. Break down your fears into smaller, manageable steps. Begin with less intimidating tasks and gradually work your way up to more challenging ones, allowing yourself to build confidence along the way.

4. Practice Relaxation Techniques: Learning relaxation techniques can help manage anxiety and stress when facing your fears. Incorporate deep breathing,

progressive muscle relaxation, or mindfulness meditation into your daily routine to calm your mind and body.

5. Seek Support: Don't hesitate to reach out for support from friends, family, or a therapist. Having someone to talk to about your fears can provide valuable perspective and encouragement. Consider joining support groups or online forums where you can connect with others facing similar challenges.

Building a Supportive Network

In the tumultuous year of 2021, marked by the heart-wrenching decline of my father due to progressive dementia, Alzheimer's, and Parkinson's; the devastating loss of my beloved sister to cancer; and the start of my journey as a single mother, my two children, Zahra and Zaheer, emerged as the pillars of strength that held me steady amidst the storm. Their unwavering support and boundless love became the guiding light that led me through the darkness, illuminating the path to healing and self-discovery.

As I embarked on my journey as a content creator on Instagram, it was Zahra and Zaheer who stood by me every step of the way; helping me script my videos, standing by me patiently through innumerable retakes, and teaching me the very basics of the platform.

Zaheer, with his keen intellect and knack for business communication, became my trusted adviser, helping me craft engaging modules for my classes and offering invaluable insights. He taught me how to look at myself as more than just an educationist. Meanwhile, Zahra's vibrant infectious enthusiasm breathed new life into my days, infusing each moment with joy and laughter. Her unwavering belief in my ability to socialise again reminded me that happiness was within reach.

From urging me to meet new people to helping me reconnect with my old friends, Zahra and Zaheer were my steadfast cheerleaders, cheering me on from the sidelines with silent thumbs-ups and reassuring smiles.

But their support extended far beyond the realms of digital content creation and socialising. Zahra and Zaheer have taken it upon themselves to tend to the small details that brought comfort and joy into my life. Whether it was stocking the fridge with my favourite chocolate ice cream or whisking me away on impromptu drives to clear my mind, they always go above and beyond to ensure that I feel loved and cared for, even in the midst of chaos.

That's why building a supportive network and surrounding ourselves with people who believe in us, challenge us, and uplift us in times of need is so important. We must cultivate meaningful relationships based on trust, empathy, and mutual respect. When we have a supportive network, we have a safe space to share our hopes, fears, and dreams, knowing that we are accepted and valued for who we are. It requires effort and intentionality. We can do this by nurturing existing relationships and seeking out new connections that align with our values and aspirations. Whether through networking events, social gatherings, or online communities; there are countless opportunities to cultivate meaningful connections that enrich our lives and bolster our self-confidence.

Ask yourself: who are the people in your life who uplift and empower you? How can you nurture and strengthen those relationships? By surrounding yourself with a supportive network, you can tackle life's challenges with confidence and resilience, knowing that you are never alone on your journey towards success and happiness.

Continuous Learning and Growth

So, here's the scoop: transitioning from the world of academia to digital content creation has been quite the ride. I mean, we're talking about going from textbooks and lecture halls to pixels and hashtags! It's been a wild journey, full of ups and downs.

I'll be honest, there have been moments where I've felt like a fish out of water. Figuring out all these new technologies and platforms felt like learning a whole new language. But you know what? I've embraced the challenge. Instead of letting those moments of self-doubt hold me back, I've taken them in stride, seeing them as opportunities to level up and grow. It's been a lesson in imperfection. I used to think I had to have it all figured out before I could make a difference. But now? I know better. I've realised that it's okay not to have all the answers, to stumble and fall along the way. What matters is picking yourself back up and keeping that fire alive.

So, yeah, I may not be a digital guru (yet!), but I'm not afraid to dive in and give it my all. Every hurdle I face is just another chance to learn and come back stronger. And hey, isn't that what life's all about?

Think about it, life's this ongoing adventure, right? And every twist and turn, every stumble and success, they're all opportunities to learn and grow. It's like saying, "Hey, bring it on, world! I'm ready for whatever you've got!" But here's the thing, continuous learning isn't just about adding new skills to your toolbox. It's about embracing this mindset where you're all about progress, not perfection. It's about seeing failure as a chance to learn, feedback as a gift, and challenges as stepping stones to becoming the best version of yourself.

So, my friend, here's your challenge: dive headfirst into this journey of continuous learning and growth. Seek out those experiences that light a fire in your soul, pursue your passions with gusto, and never, ever stop striving to be the most awesome version of you. Because when you do that, when you embrace this mindset of lifelong learning, you're unstoppable. You've got this!

Self-Acceptance in the Digital Age

When I first embarked on my digital journey, eagerly diving into the world of LinkedIn and Instagram, I was filled with excitement and anticipation. However, as I began creating content and sharing my thoughts with the world, I quickly fell into the trap of seeking validation through likes and engagement. The pressure to perform and the constant comparison to others left me feeling anxious and disheartened. It wasn't until my niece Niki and my children stepped in, reminding me to stay true to my beliefs and focus on consistency rather than metrics, that I began to find peace with myself in the digital age. Their encouragement to "post and forget" became my mantra, allowing me to embrace self-acceptance and find joy in sharing my authentic voice without being consumed by external validation.

First off, let's acknowledge that we're living in an era where everything's online. Your life, your thoughts, your breakfast – it's all out there for the world to see. And while that can be pretty cool (hello, global connection!), it also means we're bombarded with this constant stream of highlight reels from everyone else. It's easy to fall into the trap of thinking that everyone else has it all figured out. But guess what? That's just not true! Behind those perfectly curated posts, everyone's fighting their own battles, dealing with their own insecurities, and facing their struggles. So why do we put so much pressure on ourselves to measure up to these unrealistic standards?

That's where self-acceptance swoops in like a superhero. It's all about embracing who you are – the good, the bad, and the beautifully messy. But self-acceptance isn't about sitting back and saying, "Yep, this is me, take it or leave it." It's about actively choosing to love and respect yourself, even on those days when you feel like a hot mess. It's about celebrating your wins, forgiving your slip-ups, and being kind to yourself, no matter what.

So, how do we cultivate this magical thing called self-acceptance in the digital age? Well, first off, let's start by curating our online spaces like we curate our playlists – with intention. Follow accounts that inspire you, uplift you, and remind you that it's okay to be exactly who you are. And hey, if that means unfollowing that one influencer who makes you feel lousy about yourself, then so be it! Next up, let's practice some good old self-care. Yep, I'm talking about those little acts of kindness you do for yourself, whether it's taking a bubble bath, going for a walk, or binge-watching your favourite show. Because when you treat yourself with love and compassion, you're sending a powerful message to your inner critic that says, "Hey, I'm worth it." And finally, let's remember that self-acceptance is a journey, not a destination. Some days, you'll feel like you're on top of the world, and other days, you'll want to crawl under the covers and hide from the world – and that's okay! The key is to keep showing up for yourself, day after day, and to surround yourself with people who lift you up and remind you of your worth.

Here's to embracing our perfectly imperfect selves in this crazy, beautiful digital age. Let's celebrate our uniqueness, share our stories, and remember that we're all in this together.

Key Learnings

1. Embracing self-acceptance is like giving yourself a warm hug on a tough day—it's that first step towards feeling okay with who you are. It takes courage to face your insecurities head-on, but it's also a doorway to building genuine self-confidence.

2. Cultivating a growth mindset is akin to seeing obstacles as stepping stones rather than roadblocks. You must turn your "I can't" into "I'll learn." By embracing challenges, we not only conquer self-doubt but also foster resilience in the face of adversity.

3. Harnessing the power of positive self-talk is like having a cheerleader in your corner, cheering you on through life's twists and turns. By changing that inner monologue from self-criticism to self-compassion, we become better equipped to weather life's storms.

4. Confronting fears head-on and adopting gradual steps towards overcoming them enables individuals to emerge stronger and more resilient in pursuit of their goals.

5. Building a supportive network of relationships based on trust, empathy, and mutual respect fosters a sense of belonging, empowerment, and confidence in dealing with life's ups and downs.

Action Items

1. Reflect on your journey towards self-acceptance and find areas for embracing authenticity by setting aside time for introspection and journaling.

2. Practice adopting a growth mindset by seeing challenges as opportunities. Set a specific challenge for yourself each week that pushes you outside of

your comfort zone, whether it's learning a new skill or approaching a difficult conversation.

3. Integrate positive self-talk into daily routines to boost self-confidence. Create a list of go-to affirmations or mantras that resonate with you; they'll help you in challenging moments.

4. Set realistic goals that resonate with personal values and create actionable plans. Prioritise tasks based on their alignment with your values and focus on making incremental progress.

5. Embrace continuous learning and seek experiences that inspire personal development by exploring new hobbies, interests, or subjects that pique your curiosity and offer opportunities for growth.

Chapter 3

PRESSURE POINTS AND JUDGEMENT JOLTS

Have you ever felt the weight of expectation bearing down on you like a heavy load, pressing against your chest with every breath? Picture this: you're sitting in a meeting, surrounded by colleagues, the agenda buzzing around the room like an incessant fly. The conversation is lively, ideas bouncing off the walls like popcorn in a microwave. Yet, amidst this sea of chatter, you find yourself paralysed, unable to speak up. Why? Because a tiny voice in your head whispers doubts, planting seeds of insecurity that grow into towering trees of fear. It's the fear of judgement, lurking in the shadows of your mind like a relentless spectre, haunting your every move.

Now, let's rewind a bit. Think back to your childhood, those formative years when the world seemed vast and full of endless possibilities. Remember the first time you raised your hand in class, heart pounding, palms sweaty, hoping beyond hope that your answer would be met with approval rather than ridicule? Or perhaps it was during a school performance, standing under the harsh glare of the spotlight, eyes fixed on you like laser beams, as you struggled to remember your lines or hit the right notes. In those moments, the fear of judgement reared its ugly head, casting a shadow over your confidence.

Fast forward to the present day, and not much has changed, has it? Sure, the stakes may be higher now, the responsibilities greater, but the fear remains the same. It's there when you walk into a job interview, dressed to impress, yet feeling like an impostor in your own skin. It's there when you stand up to give a presentation, words stumbling over each other like clumsy dancers, as you struggle to make sense of the jumble in your mind. It's there when you share your ideas with your team, fearing rejection and criticism more than anything else.

But here's the thing: you're not alone. In fact, far from it. The fear of judgement is a universal human experience, woven into the fabric of our collective consciousness. It's what makes us human, vulnerable, imperfect. And yet, it's also what drives us to strive for greatness, to reach for the stars even when the odds are stacked against us.

As a young girl, I found myself caught in these societal expectations and cultural norms, much like many other girls around me. Growing up, I watched as my male counterparts were encouraged to pursue their passions and dreams, while I felt nudged towards a more confined, predetermined path.

While my brothers and cousins charted their own courses in life, I felt tethered to the roles prescribed for me by tradition and custom. Courses in cooking and life sciences were presented as essential skills for my future as a wife and mother, while marriage proposals loomed on the horizon, each one a reminder of the limited options laid out before me.

Yet, in the midst of these suffocating expectations, a small spark of defiance flickered within me. Despite the pressures to conform, I held onto the belief that my destiny was not predetermined by the expectations of others. Even as I entered into marriage and motherhood at a young age, I refused to let go of the dreams that whispered to me in the quiet moments of the night.

With the responsibility of caring for two young children and the weight of societal expectations bearing down on me, I realised that perseverance would be my greatest ally. In the early hours of the morning, while the world slept, I stole moments to myself to study and upskill, determined to carve out a brighter future for myself and my children.

My journey was not one of instant triumph, but rather a slow and steady process of learning and unlearning. I stumbled along the way, grappling with self-doubt and uncertainty, but with each setback, I grew stronger in my resolve to break free from the constraints of external judgement.

Through resilience and determination, I began to redefine the narrative of my life, forging a path that honoured my true desires and aspirations. And as I look back on the journey that brought me to where I stand today, I am reminded that hope exists even in the darkest of moments, and that with perseverance, we can overcome the pressures of societal expectations to create a life that is authentically our own.

So, why is it important to talk about managing pressure in personal and professional life? Because pressure is inevitable. It's the force that propels us forward, the catalyst for growth and transformation. Without pressure, we would remain stagnant, stuck in the same old patterns, doomed to repeat the same mistakes over and over again. But with pressure comes opportunity—the opportunity to rise above our fears, to challenge ourselves, to become the best versions of ourselves.

Exploring the Roots: Childhood Influences and Social Conditioning

Growing up, the seeds of fear of judgement are often sown in the fertile soil of childhood, nurtured by the expectations and perceptions of those around us. As I reflect on my own journey, I recognise the profound impact that my upbringing and societal conditioning had on shaping my perception of self and others.

From a young age, I was keenly aware of the distinct roles assigned to boys and girls within my community. While my brothers were encouraged to be assertive and ambitious, I was taught to be demure and accommodating, to prioritise the needs of others above my own. These early lessons laid the groundwork for a pervasive fear of judgement, instilling within me the belief that my worth was contingent upon meeting the expectations of those around me.

As I went through adolescence, the fear of judgement only intensified, fuelled by the unrelenting scrutiny of peers and authority figures alike. Every misstep felt like a blemish on my reputation, a mark of failure that threatened to tarnish my standing in the eyes of others. Whether it was the pressure to excel academically or the fear of social ostracisation, the spectre of judgement loomed large, casting a shadow over even the most mundane aspects of my life.

Impact of Fear of Judgement on Personal Growth and Performance

The insidious nature of the fear of judgement is its ability to seep into every facet of our lives, poisoning our thoughts and stifling our potential for growth. As I grappled with my own insecurities and doubts, I witnessed firsthand the debilitating effects of this fear on personal development and performance.

In the academic realm, the fear of judgement manifested as paralysing perfectionism, driving me to obsess over every assignment and examination for fear of falling short of expectations. Rather than viewing failure as an opportunity for growth, I internalised it as a reflection of my worth, a damning indictment of my abilities.

Similarly, in social settings, the fear of judgement acted as a barrier to authentic connection, prompting me to hide behind a facade of conformity in order to avoid scrutiny or rejection. Each interaction became a carefully choreographed dance of self-preservation, as I sought to mould around the complexities of social dynamics without revealing the vulnerabilities that lay beneath the surface.

Recognising Common Scenarios: Fear of Public Speaking, Performance Reviews, and More

One of the most common manifestations of the fear of judgement is the anxiety that accompanies public speaking, a phenomenon that many individuals, myself included, have grappled with at some point in their lives. The mere thought of standing before an audience, exposed and vulnerable, can evoke a visceral sense of dread, triggering a cascade of physiological and psychological responses that undermine performance and confidence.

Similarly, in professional settings, the fear of judgement often manifests in the form of performance reviews and evaluations, where the scope of criticism is very large. Whether it's the fear of falling short of expectations or the dread of negative feedback, the fear of judgement can cast a shadow over even the most accomplished professionals, eroding confidence and sowing seeds of self-doubt.

In recognising these common scenarios, it becomes apparent that the fear of judgement is a universal experience, one that transcends age, gender, and background. By shining a light on the roots of this fear and its impact on personal growth and performance, we can begin to unravel the tangled threads of self-doubt and insecurity, paving the way for a more authentic and empowered way of being.

Understanding the Difference Between Pressure and Stress

Today, the terms "pressure" and "stress" are often used interchangeably, but they represent distinct experiences with unique implications for personal wellbeing and performance. To deal with the complexities of pressure and stress effectively, it's essential to first understand the difference between the two.

Pressure can be defined as the external demands and expectations placed upon us, both in our personal and professional lives. These demands can take various forms, from looming deadlines at work to social obligations with friends and family. While pressure is an inevitable aspect of life, it is not inherently negative. In fact, pressure can serve as a catalyst for growth and development, pushing us to stretch beyond our comfort zones and reach new heights of achievement.

Stress arises when the demands of a situation exceed our perceived ability to cope with them effectively. Unlike pressure, which can be motivating and energising, stress is often accompanied by feelings of overwhelm, anxiety, and exhaustion. Left unchecked, chronic stress can have detrimental effects on both our physical and mental health, undermining our resilience and diminishing our capacity to perform at our best.

By recognising the distinction between pressure and stress, we can begin to reframe our relationship with external demands, viewing them not as insurmountable obstacles but as opportunities for growth and learning. Rather than succumbing to the paralysing effects of stress, we can harness the energising power of pressure to propel us forward on our personal and professional journeys.

Identifying Personal Pressure Triggers

To effectively manage pressure and leverage it for growth, it's essential to identify our individual pressure triggers—the specific situations or circumstances that evoke feelings of overwhelm. A study conducted by the American Psychological Association found that individuals frequently experience pressure when they perceive a mismatch between their behaviour and societal standards, leading to increased anxiety and self-doubt (APA, 2019). Triggers are not set in stone though; they can vary widely from person to person, depending on factors such as personality, past experiences, and current circumstances.

One afternoon, Maya, a close friend who also happens to be one of my daughter's best friends, shared her overwhelming work stress with me. Her recent promotion had brought a flood of new responsibilities and challenges. Maya expressed how she wasn't able to benefit from the promotion as she had hoped due to the stress it was causing her.

"I just can't understand how to turn this obviously amazing career move into something I actually enjoy."

According to a study published in the *Journal of Personality and Social Psychology*, individuals who fear negative evaluation often experience heightened stress levels, which can impair cognitive functions and decision-making abilities (Leary et al., 1995). That's what the core of Maya's predicament was. Reflecting on my own journey, I've come to recognise a myriad of pressure triggers that have the potential to derail my performance and hinder my personal growth. From high-stakes presentations to interpersonal conflicts and uncertainty about the future, each trigger represents a unique opportunity for self-awareness and introspection. And these aren't things you can realise overnight. I recommended that she confide in a trusted friend or family member, or consider seeking professional support, such as speaking with a therapist, since it has helped me along the way to compartmentalise my thoughts in a way that is not intimidating. She reluctantly agreed to give it a shot; two weeks later, I was sitting across a very different Maya; much calmer. Through therapy and self-introspection, she understood the exact triggers; factors like the decision-making pressure and increased team size, and above all the fear of negative evaluation, were causing all the turmoil. Once she identified the specific triggers, it was easy for her to seek help from a superior at her job, who promptly explained to her how she could streamline these processes.

By taking the time to identify our personal pressure triggers, we can begin to develop strategies for managing them effectively. Whether it's setting boundaries, practising mindfulness, or seeking support from others, understanding our triggers allows us to cultivate resilience and navigate external demands with greater ease and confidence.

Practical Tips for Managing Pressure Effectively

Incorporating practical strategies for managing pressure into our daily lives can help us build resilience and thrive in the face of adversity. Drawing on both research and personal experience, I've compiled a list of actionable tips for effectively managing pressure:

1. Prioritise self-care: In times of heightened pressure, it's crucial to prioritise self-care and activities that promote physical and mental well-being. Whether it's getting enough sleep, eating nutritious meals, or engaging in regular exercise, self-care lays the foundation for resilience and enables us to cope more effectively with external demands.

2. Practice mindfulness: Mindfulness techniques such as deep breathing, meditation, and progressive muscle relaxation can help us cultivate a sense of calm and presence in the face of pressure. By bringing our attention to the present moment, we can reduce feelings of overwhelm and enhance our capacity to respond to challenges with clarity and composure.

3. Set realistic goals: When faced with pressure, it's important to set realistic and achievable goals that align with our values and priorities. By breaking larger tasks into smaller, more manageable steps, we can avoid feeling overwhelmed and maintain a sense of momentum and progress.

4. Develop effective time management skills: Effective time management is essential for manoeuvring external demands and maximizing productivity. By prioritising tasks, setting deadlines, and minimising distractions, we can make the most of our time and minimise feelings of stress and overwhelm.

Leveraging Pressure for Personal and Professional Development

Far from being an obstacle to overcome, pressure can serve as a powerful catalyst for personal and professional development. By reframing our relationship with external demands and embracing pressure as an opportunity for growth, we can unlock our full potential and achieve success on our own terms.

In my own journey, I've experienced firsthand the transformative power of pressure, using it as a springboard for learning, growth, and self-discovery. Rather than viewing pressure as a source of stress and anxiety, I've learned to embrace it as a natural and inevitable aspect of life, one that presents endless opportunities for learning and self-improvement.

By leveraging pressure as a catalyst for personal and professional development, we can cultivate resilience, adaptability, and a sense of purpose in the face of adversity. Whether it's overcoming challenges at work, pursuing personal passions, or dealing with relationships with others, pressure can serve as a guiding force, propelling us forward on our journey toward success and fulfilment.

Key Learnings

1. The fear of judgement is a pervasive experience, rooted in childhood influences and societal conditioning, affecting personal growth and performance across various life domains.

2. Recognising common scenarios such as fear of public speaking or performance evaluations helps identify and address the fear of judgement, promoting self-awareness and resilience.

3. Distinguishing between pressure and stress is crucial for effective management, as pressure can be leveraged as a catalyst for growth, while stress can lead to negative outcomes if left unchecked.

4. Identifying personal pressure triggers enables the development of tailored strategies for managing pressure effectively, including prioritising self-care, practising mindfulness, setting realistic goals, and improving time management skills.

Action Items

1. Reflect on childhood experiences and societal influences to identify underlying fears of judgement, journaling about specific instances where judgement affected personal growth.

2. Practice exposure therapy by deliberately engaging in situations that trigger fear of judgement, such as volunteering for public speaking opportunities or actively seeking feedback from peers.

3. Develop a self-care routine that includes mindfulness practices such as meditation or deep breathing exercises, integrating them into daily activities to manage stress and promote emotional wellbeing.

4. Implement time management techniques like prioritising tasks, setting realistic deadlines, and minimising distractions to effectively manage external pressures and improve productivity.

5. Seek support from a trusted colleague or confidant. Don't hesitate to reach out for professional guidance and assistance when needed.

Chapter 4

CONNECTING BOOMERS AND ZOOMERS

Mastering communication across generations is a complex yet crucial skill in today's diverse workforce. As we explore the intricate web of intergenerational dynamics, understanding and adapting to the communication preferences of different generations becomes paramount for fostering collaboration, productivity, and harmony in the workplace.

Mastering communication across generations is essential not only in the workplace but also in personal relationships. Each generation brings its unique communication preferences, shaped by historical events, technological advancements, and societal changes. Understanding and adapting to these preferences can enhance collaboration, foster understanding, and strengthen relationships across generational divides.

Technology has significantly impacted how different generations communicate. Younger generations, especially Millennials and Gen Z, are more adept at using digital tools for communication. They often rely on social media platforms, instant messaging apps, and other online tools to stay connected. In contrast, older generations may struggle with the rapid pace of technological change and prefer more traditional forms of communication.

Source: Lenhart, A. (2015). Teens, Social Media & Technology Overview 2015. Pew Research Center. Retrieved from Pew Research Center.

Here's a guide to help you out:
Baby Boomers:

Born between 1946 and 1964, Baby Boomers grew up during a period of significant social change, including the civil rights movement, the Vietnam War, and the rise of television. As a result, they value stability, security, and traditional communication methods.

In the workplace, Baby Boomers prefer formal and structured communication settings. They thrive on face-to-face interactions and value directness and clarity in communication. Meetings, phone calls, and emails are their preferred modes of communication, as they provide a sense of familiarity and reliability. Baby Boomers appreciate being given background information and details to make informed decisions and contributions.

In personal relationships, Baby Boomers value deep and meaningful conversations. They enjoy spending quality time with family and friends, sharing stories, and reminiscing about the past. Written letters and phone calls hold sentimental value for many Baby Boomers, as they evoke a sense of nostalgia and connection.

Gen X:
Born between 1965 and 1980, Gen Xers grew up during a time of rapid technological advancement, economic uncertainty, and cultural change. Shaped by events such as the Challenger disaster and the rise of personal computers, they value independence, flexibility, and work-life balance.

In the workplace, Gen Xers prefer a work environment that emphasises individuality and autonomy. They are comfortable using various channels of communication, including email, phone calls, texts, and meetings, but they prioritise flexibility and informality. Gen Xers appreciate clear expectations and opportunities for professional development and growth.

In personal relationships, Gen Xers value authenticity and honesty. They enjoy engaging in open and candid conversations with friends and family members, discussing their thoughts, feelings, and experiences. Gen Xers are also known for their entrepreneurial spirit and creativity, often pursuing hobbies and interests outside of work.

Millennials:

Born between 1981 and 1996, Millennials came of age during the rise of the internet and digital communication technologies. They value innovation, diversity, and social responsibility, seeking meaning and purpose in both their personal and professional lives.

In the workplace, Millennials thrive in environments that prioritise collaboration, inclusivity, and flexibility. They prefer communication methods that facilitate teamwork and information sharing, such as instant messaging, video conferencing, and collaborative platforms. Millennials appreciate constructive feedback, transparency, and opportunities for growth and development.

In personal relationships, Millennials value connection and community. They are highly active on social media and digital platforms, using them to stay connected with friends, family, and peers. Millennials enjoy engaging in virtual conversations, sharing photos and updates, and participating in online communities and forums.

Gen Z:

Born between 1997 and 2012, Gen Z represents the youngest generation in the workforce and personal relationships. Growing up as digital natives, they are highly proficient in technology and value authenticity, creativity, and social justice.

In the workplace, Gen Z prefers environments that offer stability, flexibility, and opportunities for growth. They are comfortable using a wide range of communication tools, including video calls, messaging apps, and social media platforms. Gen Z values immediate feedback, clear expectations, and opportunities for skill development and advancement.

In personal relationships, Gen Z values authenticity and transparency. They enjoy engaging in real-time communication through video calls, voice messages, and social media platforms. Gen Z is highly active on platforms like Instagram, using them to express themselves creatively, connect with like-minded individuals, and advocate for causes they believe in.

Respecting Diversity and Avoiding Stereotypes

As I delve into the intricacies of communication across generations, I've come to realise that it extends far beyond merely understanding preferences. It's about respecting the diversity of perspectives and experiences within each generation. Rather than leaning on age-based stereotypes or making assumptions based on generational labels, it's crucial to approach communication with an open mind and a genuine willingness to listen and empathise with others.

Avoiding the trap of age-based stereotypes enables us to appreciate the unique contributions and viewpoints that individuals from different generations bring to the table. Instead of categorising people solely based on their age, I've learned to strive for inclusivity and create environments where everyone feels valued, respected, and heard, regardless of their generational affiliation.

Reflecting on my own journey, I recall a pivotal moment that challenged my perceptions and forced me to confront my biases about age and experience. It was during a networking event in Delhi when I encountered Jayesh, a seasoned photographer whose presence amidst a predominantly younger crowd seemed out of place.

Initially, I couldn't help but make assumptions about Jayesh based on his age. I assumed he might be out of touch with the latest trends and technologies, unable to adapt to the fast-paced world of digital content creation. However, engaging in conversation with him shattered those assumptions.

Jayesh turned out to be a treasure trove of knowledge and experience, his years in the industry lending him a depth of insight that left me in awe. He shared stories of his early days as a photographer, capturing moments of historical and cultural significance that had shaped his perspective on art and creativity. Far from being out of touch, Jayesh demonstrated a keen understanding of the digital landscape, leveraging social media and online platforms to showcase his work to a new generation of audiences.

My encounter with Jayesh was humbling and eye-opening. It made me realise how easily I had fallen into the trap of age-based stereotypes. I learned that diversity of experience and perspective knows no age limit and that true creativity transcends generational boundaries. Inspired by Jayesh's example, I made a conscious effort to challenge my own assumptions and embrace the richness of diversity in all its forms.

Understanding Communication in the Modern Digital Landscape

In today's whirlwind of digital interactions, it's no secret that effective communication is the glue holding our relationships, both personal and professional, together. Isn't it wild to think about how many text messages we read in a single day, or how much time we spend scrolling through social media? With the explosion of communication channels and platforms, mastering the art of digital communication has become more crucial than ever before. From the familiar ding of an email notification to the face-to-face connection of a video call, each digital platform offers its own set of opportunities and challenges for communication.

Clarity and Conciseness

Information overload is a common challenge today, so obviously clarity and conciseness are more important than ever. Whether you're sending an email, composing a social media post, or participating in a video conference, ensuring that your message is clear and concise is essential for effective communication. This also adequately ensures that the person you are communicating with understands the message you're trying to convey in a comprehensible manner.

Conciseness refers to expressing your ideas succinctly and efficiently, without unnecessary verbosity. In a world where attention spans are short and distractions abound, concise communication respects the recipient's time and increases the likelihood that your message will be read and understood. It also helps to keep the conversation focused and prevents information overload. At the end of the day, no one wants to read an email that feels like an essay but conveys nothing.

Importance of Clear Communication

Clear communication involves conveying your message in a way that is easily understood by the recipient. When messages are clear, there is less room for confusion or misinterpretation, leading to more productive interactions. In digital communication, where tone and body language may be absent, clarity becomes even more crucial to ensure that your intended meaning is accurately conveyed.

Tips for Clear and Concise Communication:

1. Use Plain Language: Avoid using overly technical terms or industry jargon that may be unfamiliar to your audience. Instead, opt for plain language that is accessible to everyone. Consider your audience's level of expertise and adjust your language accordingly to ensure clarity.

2. Organise Information: Structure your messages in a logical and coherent manner, with a clear introduction, body, and conclusion. Break down complex ideas into digestible chunks and use headings or bullet points to facilitate easy comprehension. By organising information effectively, you help your audience understand your message more efficiently.

3. Provide Context: Always provide sufficient context to ensure that your message is fully understood. Include

background information, relevant facts, or previous discussions that may be necessary for comprehension. By offering context, you help your audience connect the dots and grasp the significance of your message.

Let's explore these concepts further with practical examples across different digital communication platforms:

Email Communication: When composing an email, aim to keep your message concise and to the point. Start with a clear subject line that summarises the purpose of the email. An appropriate salutation sets the tone for professional communication and establishes rapport with the recipient, fostering a positive interaction from the start. This must be followed by a brief introduction and the main body of the message. Use paragraphs to break up large blocks of text and ensure that each paragraph focuses on a single idea. Finally, conclude with a call to action or a summary of key points.

Social Media Posts: Whether you're tweeting, posting on Facebook, or sharing on LinkedIn, clarity and conciseness are key to capturing your audience's attention. Craft your message carefully, keeping it short and impactful. Use hashtags sparingly and strategically to increase visibility, and include visuals such as images or videos to enhance engagement. Remember to proofread your posts for clarity and correctness before publishing.

Video Conferencing: During video conferences or virtual meetings, clarity is essential to ensure effective communication. Speak clearly and at a moderate pace, avoiding overly technical language or complex jargon. During video conferences, your appearance and surroundings play a significant role in how you are perceived by others and the effectiveness of your communication. Dress appropriately for the virtual event, considering the level of formality required. For instance, if it's an interview or a formal business meeting, opt for professional attire to convey professionalism and respect for the occasion. Additionally, pay attention to your background to ensure it is uncluttered and aesthetically pleasing. A clean and organised backdrop minimises distractions and allows participants to focus on your message. Use visual aids such as slides or screen shares to supplement your verbal communication and reinforce key points. Encourage active participation from participants by asking questions and soliciting feedback to ensure that everyone is on the same page.

Active Listening

Interactions often occur through emails, instant messages, and video conferences. The art of active listening is more important than ever. Active listening goes beyond simply hearing what others say; it involves fully engaging with the speaker, understanding their perspective, and responding thoughtfully.

Active listening is the foundation of building strong and meaningful relationships, both personally and professionally. When you actively listen to others, you demonstrate respect, empathy, and genuine interest in their thoughts and feelings. This fosters trust and rapport, leading to deeper connections and more collaborative interactions.

In digital communication, where non-verbal cues such as facial expressions and body language are often absent, active listening becomes even more crucial for understanding different perspectives. By attentively listening to what others have to say, you gain valuable insights into their viewpoints, concerns, and motivations. This enables you to respond more effectively and adapt your communication style accordingly.

Active listening has numerous benefits, including improved relationships, increased trust, and reduced misunderstandings. In professional settings, it leads to better teamwork, enhanced problem-solving, and higher productivity. It also helps in resolving conflicts by ensuring that all parties feel heard and understood.

Source: Barker, L. (2010). Listening and Speaking: Handbook of Communication Competence. Pearson.

Active listening is essential for effective problem-solving and conflict resolution. By listening attentively to all parties involved, you can identify common ground, clarify misunderstandings, and find mutually acceptable solutions. Active listening promotes open dialogue and encourages constructive communication, leading to more successful outcomes.

Tips for Practising Active Listening:
1. Give Your Full Attention: When engaging in digital communication, minimise distractions and give your full attention to the speaker. Close unnecessary tabs or applications, silence notifications, and focus on the conversation at hand. Show genuine interest in what the speaker is saying by maintaining eye contact (if on video), nodding, and providing verbal affirmations.
2. Listen Without Interrupting: Resist the urge to interrupt or interject while the speaker is talking. Instead, allow them to express their thoughts and

ideas uninterrupted. Practice patience and restraint, even if you have strong opinions or immediate responses. Remember that active listening is about understanding the speaker's perspective, not imposing your own.

3. Ask Clarifying Questions: Clarifying questions are a valuable tool for demonstrating active listening and deepening your understanding of the speaker's message. Ask open-ended questions to encourage elaboration and clarification. Summarise what you've heard to ensure that you've interpreted the speaker's words correctly. This shows that you're actively engaged and invested in the conversation.

4. Empathise and Validate: Show empathy and validation by acknowledging the speaker's emotions and experiences. Reflect their feelings back to them and validate their concerns or frustrations. This helps to create a supportive and empathetic environment where individuals feel heard and understood. Avoid dismissing or minimising their feelings, even if you disagree with their perspective.

5. Provide Constructive Feedback: After listening attentively to the speaker, provide constructive feedback that demonstrates your understanding and offers valuable insights. Avoid jumping to conclusions or making assumptions. Instead, focus on providing thoughtful feedback that addresses the speaker's concerns and contributes to the conversation constructively.

Let's explore how you can apply these principles of active listening in various digital communication scenarios:

Email Communication: When reading and responding to emails, take the time to fully understand the sender's message before crafting your response. Pay attention to the tone and context of the email, and consider the sender's perspective. Ask clarifying questions if necessary and respond thoughtfully to address their concerns or inquiries.

Texting: In instant messaging conversations, practise active listening by engaging fully with the other party's messages. Avoid multitasking or distractions while chatting and focus on the conversation at hand. Use emojis or brief responses to acknowledge the sender's messages and show that you're actively listening. You might also want to put all your thoughts into one message instead of sending out different thoughts in separate messages.

Video Conferencing: During video conferences, avoid interrupting or speaking over others and wait for your turn to contribute to the discussion. Use techniques such as paraphrasing or summarising to demonstrate your understanding and engagement.

Flexibility and Adaptability in Digital Communication

With the multitude of communication channels available, understanding how to navigate them and adapt your approach accordingly is crucial for successful interactions. Different communication channels serve distinct purposes, and selecting the appropriate channel depends on various factors such as the nature of the message, the urgency of communication, and the preferences of the audience. For example, email may be suitable for formal correspondence or documentation, while instant messaging or video conferencing may be preferable for quick discussions or collaborative meetings. Before initiating communication, consider the nature of your message and the preferences of your audience. Choose the channel that best aligns with your communication objectives and facilitates effective interaction.

With the proliferation of communication platforms, we must learn to manage multiple channels seamlessly. This requires familiarity with digital tools and the ability to transition between them effortlessly. Whether it's switching from email to instant messaging or social media to video conferencing, mastering channel navigation is essential for effective communication. Familiarise yourself with the features of different platforms and practice transitioning between them smoothly to ensure seamless communication in various contexts.

Responding to Communication Trends

As communication trends continue to evolve, it's essential to stay informed and adaptable to emerging patterns and preferences. Whether it's the growing popularity of video content, the rise of voice-activated assistants, or the increasing emphasis on visual communication, understanding these trends allows individuals to tailor their communication strategies accordingly.

Based on evolving communication trends, individuals must adapt their communication strategies to remain relevant and effective. This may involve incorporating new formats or media into your communication repertoire, such as video presentations, interactive infographics, or voice messaging. By aligning your communication strategies with current trends, you can engage your audience more effectively and stay ahead of the competition. Experiment with different communication formats and media to gauge audience response and engagement. Monitor analytics and feedback to identify successful strategies and refine your approach over time.

Overcoming Challenges and Barriers

Despite the numerous benefits of digital communication, individuals may encounter technological barriers that hinder effective interaction. Common challenges include connectivity issues, software compatibility issues, and user interface complexities. Overcoming these barriers requires patience, resourcefulness, and proactive problem-solving. Troubleshoot technical issues promptly and seek assistance from IT support or technical experts when necessary. Stay informed about software updates and improvements to minimise potential disruptions in communication.

Despite being an ICF Certified (International Coaching Federation) corporate skills expert, I've even had to adapt my approach to suit the "Insta-generation," who prefer their communication fast and snappy like a microwave meal! So, while I might be used to savouring the slow-cooked flavours of thoughtful discourse, I've learned to sprinkle a little Insta-spice into my interactions to keep up with the rapid pace of digital communication. It's like switching gears from a leisurely stroll to a high-speed race—same destination, just a different mode of transportation!

In a globalised world, digital communication often involves interactions with individuals from diverse cultural backgrounds. Understanding cultural differences requires sensitivity, empathy, and cross-cultural communication skills. Misunderstandings or misinterpretations due to cultural differences can impact relationships and collaborations, highlighting the importance of cultural competence in digital communication. Educate yourself about cultural norms, customs, and communication styles prevalent in diverse regions and communities. Approach cross-cultural interactions with an open mind and a willingness to learn from others' perspectives.

Emotional Intelligence: Nurturing Empathy in Digital Communication

When it comes to written communication, it's crucial to recognise emotional cues, respond with empathy, and cultivate emotional intelligence for meaningful connections. Let's delve into the importance of emotional intelligence in digital communication and explore practical strategies for nurturing empathy in our online interactions.

Understanding Emotional Cues

In face-to-face conversations, we can perceive the tone of voice and body language; however, interpreting emotional cues in written communication requires a different set of skills. Pay attention to subtle nuances such as word choice, punctuation, and context to decipher the underlying emotions conveyed in the message. For example, a simple change in punctuation or the use of emoticons can significantly alter the tone of a message. When reading written messages, take a moment to consider the tone and intent behind the words. Pause and reread the message if necessary to ensure accurate interpretation before responding.

When engaging with others online, strive to respond with empathy and compassion, acknowledging their emotions and validating their experiences. Whether it's offering words of encouragement, expressing understanding, or simply lending a listening ear, small gestures of empathy can make a significant difference in how others perceive and appreciate our digital interactions. Practice active listening and validation in your digital conversations by acknowledging their feelings and offering supportive responses. Remember that empathy is about being present and attuned to others' emotions, even in virtual interactions.

Cultivating Emotional Intelligence

Self-awareness is the foundation of emotional intelligence, allowing us to recognise and understand our own emotions, triggers, and communication patterns. In the digital realm, it's essential to cultivate self-awareness in various online interactions. Take time to reflect on your emotions and reactions to digital communication, identifying any patterns or tendencies that may impact your interactions with others. By becoming more self-aware, you can better regulate your emotions and communicate more authentically in the digital space. If you keep a journal or diary to record your thoughts and emotions, write down your emotions towards online interactions too. This will help you notice any recurring patterns or triggers and explore strategies for managing them effectively.

As we know, empathy is not only about understanding our own emotions but also about empathising with others and appreciating their perspectives and experiences. In the digital age, cultivating empathy allows us to build stronger connections with others and wade through diverse online communities with sensitivity and understanding. Practice putting yourself in others' shoes, considering their feelings and viewpoints before responding in digital conversations. By approaching interactions with empathy and compassion, you can create a more inclusive and supportive online environment. Engage in perspective-taking exercises by imagining yourself in someone else's position and considering how they might feel or perceive a particular situation. Actively seek out diverse perspectives and experiences to broaden your understanding and empathy in digital communication.

Respecting Privacy Boundaries

Respecting privacy boundaries entails obtaining consent before accessing or sharing someone else's personal information. Whether it's asking permission to tag someone in a photo on social media or seeking consent before sharing sensitive data in a professional context, prioritising consent demonstrates respect for individual autonomy and privacy preferences. Additionally, refraining from intrusive surveillance or monitoring practices preserves trust and fosters positive relationships in both personal and professional settings. Practice active consent in your online interactions by seeking permission before sharing personal information or engaging in data collection activities. Respect others' privacy preferences and boundaries, and communicate transparently about how their information will be used and protected.

Key Learnings

1. Recognising and adjusting to how different generations communicate is key for better teamwork and harmony, both at work and in personal connections.
2. Every generation, from Baby Boomers to Gen Z, has its own unique way of communicating, influenced by the times they grew up in and the tech available.
3. Valuing diversity means appreciating the varied perspectives each generation brings, without relying on stereotypes.
4. Mastering digital communication involves being clear, concise, and empathetic while respecting privacy boundaries.
5. Embracing a mindset of growth, staying open to new ideas, and committing to ongoing learning is vital for thriving in today's fast-paced digital world.

Action Items

1. Reflect on your own communication style and identify areas where you can adapt to accommodate different generational preferences, whether in the workplace or personal relationships.
2. Look for workshops, webinars, or seminars focused on intergenerational communication. Many organisations offer training sessions specifically designed to help individuals understand communication preferences across different generations.
3. Practice simplifying your messages and providing context in your digital conversations to ensure clarity.

4. Pay attention to how people from different generations communicate in various settings, such as meetings, social gatherings, or online forums. Observe their language, tone, and nonverbal cues to gain a better understanding of their communication styles.

Chapter 5

PATHFINDING

Life is a journey filled with twists, turns, and unexpected detours. It's a voyage that often leads us through uncharted territory, presenting us with challenges and opportunities along the way. This journey, marked by significant transitions, is what I like to call pathfinding – the art of dealing with life's changes with resilience and adaptability.

But why are these transitions so important? Why do we need to embrace them rather than resist them? The answer lies in the very nature of life itself. Change is inevitable. It's a fundamental aspect of the human experience, woven into the fabric of our existence. From the moment we are born until the day we take our last breath, we are constantly evolving, growing, and transforming.

Transitions are the catalysts for this evolution. They force us to confront new realities, to challenge our assumptions, and to stretch beyond our comfort zones. Without these transitions, we would remain stagnant, stuck in the same patterns and routines, never fully realising our potential.

But embracing change is easier said than done. It requires courage, resilience, and a willingness to let go of the familiar and embrace the unknown. It means stepping into uncertainty with an open heart and a curious mind, ready to explore new possibilities and discover hidden strengths.

Losing my dad and my sister, especially to such heartbreaking circumstances, felt like losing my anchors, my constants in a world that often felt uncertain and overwhelming. They were more than just family; they were my pillars of support, my confidants, my guiding lights. When they were suddenly taken from me, it felt like the ground had been pulled out from beneath my feet, leaving me adrift in a sea of grief and uncertainty.

My dad, though physically present, was no longer the man I once knew. Progressive dementia and Alzheimer's had robbed him of his ability to communicate, to recognise his loved ones, and to care for himself. He is now under 24/7 care, his once vibrant personality reduced to a mere shadow of its former self. He had always been my rock, my source of wisdom and guidance, but now I find myself facing a future without his counsel and support.

Similarly, losing my sister to cancer was a devastating blow. She had been more than just a sister to me; she was my closest friend, my confidante, my partner in crime. We shared everything – from late-night chats about life to shopping trips and girly gossip sessions. Losing her meant losing not only a sister but also a friend, a companion, a soulmate.

In the aftermath of these circumstances, I found myself consumed by grief and despair. I didn't want to face the world; I wanted to retreat into myself, to shut out the pain and pretend like none of it had ever happened. But deep down, I knew that wasn't the answer. I knew that if I wanted to honour the good memories we all shared and find a way forward, I would need to summon the courage to confront my pain head-on and embrace the changes that lay ahead.

It wasn't easy, and there were many moments when I felt like giving up. But gradually, I began to realise that their absence, as devastating as it is, also presented me with an opportunity – an opportunity to rediscover myself, to redefine my identity, and to forge a new path forward. I started by acknowledging my own worth and value, something I had neglected for far too long. For years, I had put the needs of others before my own, always prioritising their happiness and wellbeing over my own. But in the wake of my losses, I realised that I needed to start taking care of myself – emotionally, physically, and mentally.

I also began to take steps towards reclaiming my independence and autonomy. I educated myself on financial matters, learning how to manage my dad's affairs and make informed decisions about investments and property. It was a steep learning curve, and there were many moments of frustration and self-doubt. But with each small victory, I gained a newfound sense of confidence and empowerment. Slowly but surely, I began to rebuild my life, one step at a time. I surrounded myself with supportive friends and family who lifted me up and encouraged me to keep moving forward. I explored new interests and hobbies, rediscovering passions that had long been buried beneath the weight of my grief.

And as I went through this journey of self-discovery and healing, I came to realise that resilience isn't about bouncing back to the way things were before. It's about embracing the changes and challenges that life throws our way and finding the strength within ourselves to keep moving forward, even when the path ahead seems uncertain.

In the end, my losses taught me that change is inevitable, but growth is optional. It's up to each of us to choose how we respond to life's challenges – whether we shrink back in fear or rise up with courage and resilience. And while the road ahead may be long and difficult, I take comfort in knowing that I have the strength and resilience to face whatever lies ahead, one step at a time.

Here's what you can do when you're in such times of transition:

Acknowledge Your Feelings

Life transitions can evoke a complex mix of emotions. When confronting significant changes, such as embarking on a new career, relocating to a new city, or dealing with a loss, it's entirely normal to experience a wide range of feelings. You might feel exhilarated by new opportunities yet simultaneously anxious about uncertainties. You may feel sorrow for what you're leaving behind while holding hope for the future. In the midst of these emotions, a sense of uncertainty often prevails, leaving you unsure of how to tread the path ahead.

During such times, it's vital to acknowledge and honour your emotions. Take a moment to pause and reflect on what you're experiencing. Are you feeling apprehensive about the future? Are you mourning the loss of what you're leaving behind? Are you feeling a spark of excitement about the new possibilities? Whatever you're feeling, recognise that these emotions are valid and understandable.

Grant yourself the permission to experience these emotions without judgement. It's common to dismiss or suppress feelings, believing that we should be stronger or more resilient. However, embracing your emotions is a sign of strength, not weakness. Emotions are an intrinsic part of the human experience, and denying them only delays the healing process.

Embrace your feelings, whatever they may be. If you feel sad, allow yourself to cry. If you're anxious, acknowledge your fears rather than pushing them away. If you're excited, lean into that excitement and embrace the future's possibilities. After losing my sister, I often confined myself to my room, unable to leave my bed. To the outside world, it might have seemed like I was wallowing in grief, but I needed that phase. It was the first and most crucial step in healing: allowing myself to feel.

By acknowledging and honouring your emotions, you're taking a significant step towards self-awareness and emotional healing. It's perfectly okay not to have everything figured out immediately. Transitions take time, and it's essential to give yourself the space and grace. Be gentle with yourself and remember that you are not alone in this journey.

Reframe Your Perspective

As I stood backstage at the Google for Education event, my heart was racing, and my palms were clammy with nerves. I had been invited to give a speech on the importance of education in front of some of the most influential figures in the tech industry and the education sector. It was an incredible opportunity, but it also filled me with a sense of dread.

Leading up to the event, I found myself consumed by anxiety. The weight of expectations felt heavy on my shoulders, and the fear of stumbling over my words or failing to make an impact gnawed at me. Despite long hours of preparation and practice, I couldn't shake off the feeling of impostor syndrome that seemed to loom over me like a dark cloud.

In the days leading up to the event, I confided in my therapist friend Sophia Peermohideen (Founder of Mind Wellness Center and Clinical Psychologist). She listened patiently as I poured out my fears and doubts, allowing me to voice my anxieties without judgement. Instead of what I told, which was to simply "get over it," she offered me a different perspective – one that would ultimately change the way I approached the challenge ahead.

She reminded me that moments of transition and change are often accompanied by feelings of discomfort and uncertainty. Instead of resisting these emotions, she encouraged me to embrace them as opportunities for growth and self-discovery. It was a perspective shift that would profoundly alter the way I approached the challenges that lay ahead. Her words resonated with me, prompting me to reframe my perspective on the situation. Instead of berating myself for feeling anxious, I chose to see my nerves as a sign that I was invested in the outcome.

I reminded myself that it was okay to be nervous and that I didn't have to be perfect to make an impact. Armed with this mindset, I stepped onto the stage with a renewed sense of confidence. As I delivered my speech, I focused not on the fear of failure but on the opportunity to share my passion for education with an audience that was eager to listen. I spoke from the heart, drawing on personal anecdotes and insights to connect with my audience on a deeper level.

To my surprise, the speech flowed effortlessly, and the words seemed to pour out of me with ease. In that moment, I realised that my anxiety had transformed into fuel, propelling me forward and driving me to deliver a performance that exceeded my own expectations. As I stepped off the stage to applause, I felt a sense of pride wash over me. I had faced my fears head-on and emerged victorious, proving to myself that I was capable of rising to the challenge. And while the nerves had never truly disappeared, I had learned to embrace them as a natural part of the journey, rather than allowing them to hold me back.

Reflecting on that experience, I see how it embodies the essence of pathfinding – the art of navigating life's transitions with courage and resilience. In embracing the unknown, I had discovered hidden reserves of strength and resilience, proving to myself that I was capable of facing whatever challenges life may throw my way. And while the journey had been fraught with uncertainty, it had ultimately led me to a place of growth and self-discovery.

Cultivate Resilience

Imagine standing at a crossroads, the path ahead shrouded in uncertainty. It's a familiar feeling, isn't it? That moment when you're faced with a decision that could alter the course of your life. For me, those moments have been plentiful, each one presenting its own set of challenges and opportunities. But amidst the chaos and confusion, there's one thing I've learned to rely on – resilience.

Yes, you hear about resilience all the time. But what is it? Resilience isn't something you're born with; it's a skill, a muscle that needs to be exercised and strengthened over time. It's about bouncing back from adversity, finding the courage to face life's challenges head-on, and emerging stronger than before. But how do you cultivate resilience, especially when you find yourself at a crossroads?

First and foremost, cultivating resilience begins with embracing the inevitability of change. Change is a constant in life, an ever-present force that shapes our experiences and moulds our identities. And yet, so often, we resist change, clinging to the familiar and the comfortable, even when it no longer serves us. But the truth is, change is inevitable – it's how we respond to it that matters most. For example, yes, I was stuck in my room, lying in bed, trying to cope with my grief in some way. But eventually, I had to drag myself out, not just because I had the responsibilities of an entire family on my shoulders, but also because I felt a gnawing sense that staying in bed, shut off from the world, wouldn't make things any easier. I let myself feel my feelings, got back up, dusted myself off and got to work. I had a choice – I could let this tragedy define me, or I could use it as an opportunity to grow and evolve.

Slowly, I began to embrace the changes that had been thrust upon me. I allowed myself to feel the full spectrum of emotions – the sadness, the anger, the heartache – without judgement or resistance. And in doing so, I discovered a strength within myself that I never knew existed.

To truly cultivate resilience, you must also learn to adapt and thrive in the face of uncertainty. This means being willing to step outside of your comfort zone, to take risks, and to embrace the unknown with an open heart and mind. For me, this meant learning to let go of my need for control and certainty, and instead, learning to trust in the process of life. It meant being willing to try new things, even if they scared me, and being open to the possibility of failure. And most importantly, it meant cultivating a sense of curiosity and wonder about the world around me, embracing each new experience as an opportunity for growth and learning.

As I reflect on my own journey of cultivating resilience, one particular challenge stands out as a defining moment in my pathfinding quest. It was a time when I made a conscious decision to reclaim control over my life, to undo everything that had shattered my confidence and left me feeling adrift in a sea of uncertainty. Physically, I embarked on a journey of transformation, determined to shed the weight—both literal and metaphorical—that had been holding me back. I joined the gym with a newfound sense of purpose, pushing myself to new limits and shedding fourteen kilos along the way. What had initially started as a means to improve my physical health soon became a lifestyle. Since evenings were the toughest, the gym became a crucial filler, providing me with an endorphin rush that helped me feel calm and centred. With every workout, I reminded myself, "I will make it through this." Losing the weight was just a bonus; the real victory was regaining my sense of self and resilience.

But resilience, I soon realised, was not just about physical strength; it was about cultivating mental fortitude in the face of adversity. Despite my initial hesitation, I pushed myself to step outside of my comfort zone and socialise more. I eventually found a sense of belonging and purpose as a member of the esteemed Rotary Club of Bombay Bayview.

Even academically, I challenged myself to reach new heights. Despite already holding double Masters in Education and English Literature, I set my sights on a prestigious goal: Harvard Graduate School of Education

(HGSE). The journey was arduous, but with unwavering determination and relentless effort, I cracked the interview and earned a coveted spot at HGSE. Through these accomplishments, I came to understand that true resilience is not measured by external achievements or accolades. It is forged in the fires of adversity, strengthened by the trials and tribulations of life.

No amount of success or physical fitness can compensate for a lack of mental resilience. It was a realisation that hit home when my children sat me down and gently urged me to seek help from a therapist when they saw me compensating for my grief rather than healing from it. They reminded me that true happiness and resilience could only come from within, that I held the remote control to my own wellbeing. It was a humbling moment, but also a profound one – a reminder that cultivating resilience is not just about overcoming external challenges, but about nurturing inner strength and resilience.

Opening up to a trained professional was one of the best decisions I ever made. My therapist helped me unpack my thoughts and emotions, offering me a safe space to explore my fears and insecurities. Through our sessions, I gained valuable insights and coping strategies that helped me face the challenges I was facing with greater resilience and self-awareness. But seeking support doesn't always mean turning to professionals. Sometimes, it's as simple as reaching out to a friend or loved one and letting them know you're struggling. I can't tell you how many times a conversation with a friend has helped me gain perspective on a challenging situation or offered me the encouragement and support I needed to keep going.

In addition to seeking support from others, it's also important to cultivate a strong sense of self-compassion. Self-compassion is the practice of treating yourself with kindness, understanding, and acceptance – especially in moments of struggle or suffering. It's about extending the same level of care and compassion to yourself that you would to a dear friend in need.

During times of change and transition, it's easy to be hard on ourselves. We might berate ourselves for not having all the answers or for making mistakes along the way. But practising self-compassion reminds us that we're only human – imperfect, fallible, and deserving of love and understanding. It starts with paying attention to the way you talk to yourself. Are you kind and supportive, or are you harsh and critical? If you find yourself engaging in negative self-talk, try to reframe your thoughts and speak to yourself with kindness and compassion.

One strategy that has been particularly helpful for me is the practice of self-affirmations. These are positive statements that you can repeat to yourself to challenge negative self-talk and cultivate a sense of self-worth and confidence. For example, instead of telling yourself "I'm not good enough," try saying "I am worthy of love and respect." A personal affirmation that I like to use is:

"I am love, I am light, I am magic. I attract the right people and the right opportunities in my life."

Finally, cultivating resilience also requires a willingness to learn and grow from your experiences. This means being open to feedback, admitting when you're wrong, and proactively seeking opportunities for both personal and professional development. Whether you're a student, a teen, or a young married adult, challenges and expectations are inevitable. Resilience is not something that will leave you; it will be with you through all stages of life. Embrace it as an ally rather than villainising it. Befriend resilience, and it will support you in dealing with life's ups and downs with strength and grace.

Key Learnings

1. Life is filled with inevitable changes and transitions. Embracing these shifts, rather than resisting them, allows for personal growth and transformation.

2. Reframe Your Perspective: Shifting your mindset from fear and anxiety to opportunities for growth can transform how you approach and overcome challenges.

3. Resilience is a skill that can be developed over time through self-compassion, seeking support, and embracing new experiences with an open mind.

Action Items

1. Choose a few positive affirmations that resonate with you and repeat them daily. This can help shift your mindset and build self-confidence. For example, "I am worthy of love and respect" or "I have the strength to face life's challenges."

2. Identify a goal that excites you, whether it's academic, career-related, or personal. For instance, I aimed for Harvard despite already holding double masters. Set your sights on something you're passionate about, make a plan, and take steps towards achieving it. This can provide a sense of direction and purpose.

3. Assemble a collection of strategies, resources, and activities that help you manage stress and stay grounded during difficult times. This might include mindfulness exercises, favourite inspirational quotes, contact information for supportive friends, or activities that bring you joy and relaxation. Use this toolkit whenever you feel overwhelmed or in need of a boost.

Chapter 6

THE SOCIAL MAZE

Picture this: You're at a party, surrounded by a sea of unfamiliar faces and chattering voices. Your heart starts racing, your palms get sweaty, and you can feel the familiar pang of anxiety creeping up on you. All you want to do is disappear into the nearest corner and hope no one notices you. If this scenario sounds all too familiar, you're not alone.

Today, social skills are more important than ever. They're the building blocks of meaningful relationships, successful careers, and overall wellbeing. But for many of us, traversing social situations can feel like traversing a minefield – filled with uncertainty, self-doubt, and fear of judgement. In this chapter, we'll delve deep into the world of social skills, exploring what they are, why they're important, and most importantly, how you can master them. From understanding the root causes of social anxiety to learning practical strategies for improving your social interactions, we'll cover it all.

Understanding Social Anxiety

Social anxiety – it's a term that's thrown around a lot, but what does it really mean? Imagine walking into a room full of people and feeling like all eyes are on you, scrutinising your every move. Your mind starts racing with thoughts of inadequacy and judgement, and before you know it, you're paralysed with fear.

Social anxiety is more than just feeling shy or nervous in social situations. It's a pervasive fear of embarrassment, rejection, or negative evaluation by others. In extreme cases, it can even manifest in physical symptoms like sweating, trembling, and a rapid heartbeat, making even the simplest interactions feel like insurmountable challenges. A nationwide survey conducted by the National Institute of Mental Health and Neurosciences (NIMHANS) in India highlighted that a significant portion of the population suffers from social anxiety disorder. The study emphasised that many cases go undiagnosed due to stigma and a lack of awareness (NIMHANS, 2020).

In the United States, data from the National Comorbidity Survey Replication (NCS-R) revealed that an estimated 7.1% of adults aged 18 or older, experienced social anxiety disorder in the past year.

But here's the thing – social anxiety is not a life sentence. It's a common struggle that a large number of people face, and it's entirely possible to overcome. By understanding the root causes of your anxiety and learning effective coping strategies, you can take back control of your social life and thrive in any situation.

The Importance of Social Skills

Now, that we've tackled the elephant in the room, let's talk about why social skills are so darn important. Think of social skills as the glue that holds our social fabric together – they're the invisible threads that connect us to others and help us manoeuvre the complexities of human interaction. From landing your dream job to finding your soulmate, social skills play a crucial role in every aspect of life. They enable us to communicate effectively and build meaningful relationships in the ever-changing landscape of social norms and expectations. In short, they're the secret sauce to success and happiness.

But here's the kicker – social skills aren't just about making small talk or cracking jokes at parties (although those certainly help). They're also about understanding emotions, showing empathy, and resolving conflicts in a constructive manner. In other words, they're the foundation of healthy relationships and emotional intelligence.

Social situations can sometimes feel like a minefield, with potential pitfalls at every turn. But fear not, because mastering social skills is not only possible, but it can also be a game-changer in both your personal and professional life. In this section, we'll explore some key areas for improving your social skills, from starting conversations and making small talk to assertiveness and setting boundaries, and understanding the nuances of nonverbal communication and body language.

Starting Conversations and Making Small Talk

Ah, the dreaded small talk – the bane of introverts and the cornerstone of social interactions. But fear not, because making small talk doesn't have to be as painful as pulling teeth. In fact, with a few simple strategies up your sleeve, you can turn small talk into an art form.

First things first, let's talk about starting conversations. It's easy to feel tongue-tied when approaching someone new, but remember – everyone loves to talk about themselves. So why not break the ice with a simple question or observation? Whether it's commenting on the weather, complimenting someone's outfit, or asking about their weekend plans, a little bit of small talk can go a long way in forging connections.

But here's the key – small talk is just the tip of the iceberg. Once you've broken the ice, it's time to dive deeper and find common ground. Ask open-ended questions that invite meaningful conversation, and listen actively to what the other person has to say. Remember, the goal is not just to fill the silence, but to create a genuine connection with the people around you.

Assertiveness and Boundary Setting

Now let's talk about assertiveness and boundary setting – two essential skills for navigating social situations with confidence and grace. Assertiveness is all about expressing your thoughts, feelings, and needs in a clear and respectful manner, without being aggressive or passive. It's about standing up for yourself and advocating for your own interests, while also respecting the rights and boundaries of others.

Setting boundaries is closely related to assertiveness, and it's equally important in maintaining healthy relationships. Boundaries are like invisible fences that define what is and isn't acceptable in your interactions with others. Whether it's saying no to unreasonable demands, asserting your personal space, or standing up against disrespect, setting boundaries is crucial for protecting your wellbeing and preserving your self-respect.

But here's the thing – asserting yourself and setting boundaries can be easier said than done, especially if you're used to putting other people's needs ahead of your own. It takes practice and courage to speak up for yourself and assert your boundaries, but trust me when I say this – the payoff is well worth the effort. So don't be afraid to assert yourself and set clear boundaries in your interactions with others – your happiness and wellbeing depend on it.

Nonverbal Communication and Body Language

Now let's talk about the silent language of nonverbal communication and body language. Did you know that up to 93% of communication is nonverbal? That's right – your body language speaks volumes, even when you're not saying a word. A study by the Indian Institute of Management (IIM) Bangalore emphasised the importance of understanding facial expressions in cross-cultural communication, especially in a diverse country like India where expressions may vary between regions (IIM Bangalore, 2020).

From the way you stand to the way you gesture, your body language can convey a wealth of information about your thoughts, feelings, and intentions. By learning to read and interpret nonverbal cues, you can gain valuable insights into the people around you and adjust your own behaviour accordingly.

But it's not just about decoding nonverbal cues – it's also about mastering your own body language to convey confidence, warmth, and authenticity. Here are some actionable steps to help you interpret and use nonverbal cues to your advantage:

1. Learn the Basics: Familiarise yourself with common nonverbal cues and their meanings. For example, crossed arms may indicate defensiveness or resistance, or even a "my way or the highway" attitude; while open palms suggest honesty and openness. Understanding these basics can help you interpret others' body language more accurately.

2. Observe Others: Take note of how people around you use their body language in different situations. Notice

their posture, facial expressions, gestures, and tone of voice. Pay attention to how these nonverbal cues align with their verbal messages, as they can often provide additional context or insight.

3. Mirror and Match: Mirroring is a technique where you subtly mimic the body language of the person you're interacting with. This can create a sense of rapport and connection, as it signals that you're on the same wavelength. However, be careful not to overdo it or appear insincere.

4. Maintain Eye Contact: Eye contact is a powerful nonverbal cue that conveys confidence, attentiveness, and sincerity. When speaking with someone, maintain comfortable eye contact to show that you're engaged and interested in the conversation. Avoid staring, as it can come across as aggressive or intimidating.

5. Use Open Body Language: Project confidence and approachability by adopting open body language. Stand or sit up straight, uncross your arms, and maintain a relaxed posture. Avoid fidgeting or crossing your legs, as these behaviours can signal nervousness or discomfort.

So, the next time you find yourself in a social situation, pay attention to the silent language of nonverbal communication and body language. By mastering these subtle cues, you can become a more effective communicator and forge deeper connections with the people around you.

Social situations can be both exciting and challenging. Whether you're attending a networking event, gathering with friends and family, in romantic relationships, or dealing with conflict and rejection, each scenario presents its own set of opportunities and obstacles. We'll explore each of these social situations in detail, providing practical tips and strategies to help you navigate them with confidence and ease.

Networking Work Events and Professional Settings

Networking events and professional settings can initially feel daunting, especially when meeting new people or striving to make a memorable impression. However, with the right mindset and approach, these occasions can transform into invaluable opportunities for professional growth and meaningful connections.

Approach these events with clear objectives in mind, whether it's forging new relationships, exploring career opportunities, or gleaning insights from industry experts. Having a well-defined purpose will help you go through the event with focus and direction, ensuring you make the most of the experience. Preparation is key to success at networking events. Take the time to research the event beforehand, familiarising yourself with the attendees, speakers, and topics that will be covered. Armed with this knowledge, you can tailor your conversations and questions to align with the interests and expertise of those you'll be engaging with. But simply knowing who will be there and what will be discussed is not enough. Remember, you're there to network and grow professionally. You can't just linger on the sidelines. An elevator pitch is the perfect tool to help you make a strong start.

Crafting a compelling elevator pitch is akin to preparing your secret weapon. This succinct and persuasive speech outlines who you are, what you do, and what makes you unique or valuable, all within the span of a brief elevator ride – typically around 30 seconds to 2 minutes. The significance of an elevator pitch lies in its ability to quickly and effectively communicate your personal brand or professional identity in a memorable and engaging manner, especially in professional networking scenarios. It serves as your introduction to others, leaving a positive and lasting first impression, and setting the tone for further interactions. In crafting your elevator pitch for your personal brand, it's crucial to include three key components:

1. What makes you unique: Highlight the distinctive qualities, skills, and experiences that set you apart from others in your field. Whether it's your innovative approach to problem-solving, your unique perspective on industry trends, or your diverse background and expertise, emphasise what makes you stand out and capture the listener's attention.

2. What makes you valuable: Clearly communicate the value you bring to the table and how your unique qualities translate into tangible benefits for others. Whether it's your ability to drive results, your track record of success, or your exceptional customer service skills, emphasise how you can solve problems, meet needs, or create opportunities for those you engage with.

3. What your goals are: Articulate your professional aspirations, objectives, and vision for the future. Whether you're seeking new career opportunities, looking to expand your network, or aiming to make a meaningful impact in your industry, share your goals

with clarity and enthusiasm, demonstrating your ambition and drive.

By incorporating these elements into your elevator pitch, you can effectively communicate your personal brand in a concise and compelling way, leaving a positive and memorable impression on those you meet and opening doors to new opportunities for growth and success. Moreover, opportunities can arise unexpectedly, and having a well-prepared elevator pitch enables you to capitalise on these moments.

Approachability is like the key that unlocks the door to meaningful connections. As you begin to explore the room, don't underestimate the power of a warm smile and a confident handshake. These simple gestures can speak volumes, instantly putting others at ease and signalling your openness to conversation. Imagine extending your hand with a genuine smile, feeling the connection as you make eye contact and exchange pleasantries. It's a small moment, but it sets the stage for genuine interaction.

Now, let's talk about the art of conversation. Open-ended questions are your secret weapon, inviting others to share their experiences and insights in a way that fosters deeper connection. Instead of sticking to small talk, consider asking questions that spark meaningful dialogue. For example, you might inquire about someone's professional journey, their passions outside of work, or their thoughts on industry trends. By demonstrating genuine interest and curiosity, you create an environment where conversation can flourish.

But the magic doesn't stop there. Seizing the opportunity to exchange contact information ensures that your connection doesn't end when the event does. Whether it's swapping business cards or connecting on LinkedIn, nurturing these connections beyond the initial interaction is crucial. Imagine exchanging contact information with someone you've connected with, excited about the potential for future collaboration or mentorship. By staying proactive and engaged, you lay the foundation for lasting relationships that can benefit both parties professionally.

After the event winds down and you head home, your networking journey is far from over. In fact, it's just beginning. The next crucial step is to follow up with the people you met, turning those initial connections into lasting relationships. I remember attending a networking event at the Global Chambers in Churchgate, where I had the pleasure of meeting the author of the book Human Connect, Manoj Gursahani. People were exchanging their business cards left and right, but it made me wonder how many of those cards would actually be remembered and how many would end up in the dustbin.

As I stood there, I noticed how first impressions can easily become lasting impressions if not handled thoughtfully. How one speaks and connects is what truly matters. I made sure to engage Manoj in a meaningful conversation, discovering our shared interests in the field of education. We connected on social media, but it was the depth of our conversation that made a lasting impact. The next day, I sat down at my desk, coffee in hand, ready to dive into my inbox. Among the messages and notifications, I spotted the names of the individuals I had connected with, including Manoj. It was time to craft personalised messages expressing my gratitude for our conversation and my genuine interest in staying connected.

When I reached out to Manoj on LinkedIn, he instantly remembered me from our discussion. It was clear that the way we connected over shared interests had made a significant impression. This experience taught me that while exchanging business cards and contact information is important, the real key to lasting connections lies in the quality of the interactions and the follow-up. As you type out each message, reflect on the conversations you've had and the insights you've gained. Maybe you bonded over a shared passion for sustainability or exchanged ideas about the future of your industry. Whatever the connection, let it shine through in your follow-up message. Craft a thoughtful message that highlights the specific points you discussed and expresses your enthusiasm for continuing the conversation. By taking the time to personalise each message, you show that you value the connection and are invested in nurturing it further.

But don't stop there. Take it a step further by offering to meet for coffee or scheduling a follow-up call. Imagine extending the invitation, suggesting a time and place to reconvene and dive deeper into the topics you explored together. Whether it's a cosy coffee shop downtown or a virtual meeting over Zoom, the goal is the same: to continue building rapport and exploring shared interests. By offering to meet again, you demonstrate your commitment to fostering meaningful connections and investing in professional relationships.

Gatherings with Friends and Family

Gatherings with friends and family are indeed special occasions, woven with threads of laughter, shared memories, and cherished moments. Whether it's a cosy dinner party at a friend's place or a lively family reunion in the backyard, these gatherings offer a precious opportunity to reconnect with the people who matter most in our lives. I make it a point to gather my family at my place every few weeks. The aroma of home-cooked meals fills the air as we hug and greet each other with smiles and laughter. It's always a scene straight out of a feel-good movie – everyone catching up, sharing stories, and simply enjoying each other's company.

But participating in these social gatherings isn't just about showing up – it's about being present and engaged in the moment. Sitting around the dinner table, passing dishes of delicious food, and clinking glasses in a toast to friendship and togetherness, I realised the importance of actively participating in the conversations, sharing my own experiences, and listening attentively to others.

Of course, these gatherings can also present challenges, from sensitive topics popping up to managing different personalities. However, with patience, empathy, and understanding, we can overcome these challenges, fostering deeper connections and stronger relationships in the process. There's always banter in gatherings like these; some can even turn into debates about opposing opinions in politics, art, and more.

In moments like these, I've learned the importance of approaching the situation with an open mind and a willingness to listen. Listening is crucial because it shows respect for the other person's perspective and can defuse tension. Instead of trying to win the argument, shift the focus to finding common ground and mutual respect. Actively listening, rather than waiting for your turn to speak, allows you to understand where the other person is coming from. This approach can transform a heated debate into a productive and enlightening conversation.

After all, at the end of the day, you'd much rather be smiling about the great conversation and good food than sulking about some silly argument. By prioritising listening and understanding over winning, you foster an environment where everyone feels heard and valued, which is the foundation of strong and meaningful connections. Let's not forget the joy of creating memorable experiences together. Whether it's organising a game night with friends or planning a family outing to the beach, these shared activities create opportunities for bonding and laughter. From engaging in late-night board games to sharing meaningful conversations with loved ones – these moments create lasting memories and deepen the bonds of friendship and family.

In essence, gatherings with friends and family are a celebration of the connections that enrich our lives. They remind us of the importance of community, laughter, and love, offering a refuge from the hustle and bustle of everyday life. So, the next time you find yourself surrounded by the people you hold dear, take a moment to savour the magic of the moment and cherish the bonds that unite us all (and put your phones away for a bit!)

Nurturing Connections – Communication in Relationships

Effective communication forms the bedrock of any meaningful relationship. It's the bridge that connects individuals, allowing them to share their thoughts, feelings, and experiences with one another. Whether it's expressing love and affection or resolving conflicts, communication is the key to building trust, intimacy, and mutual respect.

In a world where social media often encourages curated personas and filtered images, authenticity stands out as a rare and precious commodity. Being true to yourself and embracing your quirks and imperfections can foster genuine connections with others. Instead of putting on a facade or trying to impress, authenticity invites others to see you for who you truly are, creating a foundation of trust and openness in your relationships.

Communication is a two-way street, requiring not only the ability to express oneself but also the willingness to listen attentively to others. Active listening involves more than just hearing words; it's about fully engaging with the speaker, empathising with their emotions, and validating their experiences. By practising active listening, you demonstrate respect and empathy, paving the way for deeper understanding and connection in your relationships. Sometimes, communication can make you feel quite vulnerable, and that's just part of the process. Vulnerability is often misunderstood as a sign of weakness, but in reality, it is a profound act of courage and strength. Opening up and sharing your true thoughts and feelings with others can be daunting, but it's also incredibly liberating. Vulnerability fosters intimacy and trust, allowing you to forge deep connections with others based on authenticity and mutual understanding.

Every relationship comes with its own set of challenges, and challenges generally result in conflict. Conflict is a natural part of any relationship, but it's how you communicate through disagreements that determines the health and longevity of the relationship. Instead of avoiding conflict or resorting to destructive communication patterns, strive to resolve conflicts constructively. This involves active listening, expressing your feelings without blame or judgement, and seeking mutually acceptable solutions through compromise and understanding. Empathy plays a crucial role in fostering meaningful connections with others. By putting yourself in the shoes of others and viewing situations from their perspective, you can cultivate empathy and understanding in your relationships. This helps bridge differences, promote mutual respect, and strengthen bonds of trust and compassion.

Key Learnings:

1. Social anxiety is a common struggle that many people face, but it's possible to overcome it by understanding its root causes and learning effective coping strategies. By taking control of your social anxiety, you can thrive in social situations and build meaningful connections with others.

2. Social skills are essential for success in both personal and professional life. They enable us to communicate effectively, build relationships, and navigate social norms and expectations. From making small talk to setting boundaries, mastering social skills can open doors to opportunities and enhance overall wellbeing.

3. Assertiveness and boundary setting are crucial for maintaining healthy relationships. Assertiveness allows you to express your thoughts and needs respectfully, while setting boundaries protects your wellbeing and preserves self-respect. By practising assertiveness and boundary setting, you can deal with social situations with confidence and grace.

4. Nonverbal communication and body language play a significant role in social interactions. Understanding and mastering these subtle cues can enhance your communication skills and help you forge deeper connections with others. From maintaining eye contact to using open body language, small adjustments can make a big difference in how you are perceived by others.

Action Items

1. Experiment with different conversation starters and icebreakers to make small talk more engaging

and enjoyable. Keep in mind that genuine curiosity and empathy are key ingredients for meaningful conversations.

2. Take note of your own body language and nonverbal cues during social interactions. Practice mirroring and matching the body language of others to establish rapport and connection. Pay attention to how subtle changes in your body language can impact the dynamics of a conversation.

3. Start with small, low-stakes scenarios to build your assertiveness skills. For instance, express your preference when choosing a restaurant or movie with friends. Gradually work your way up to more challenging situations where asserting your needs and boundaries is crucial.

Chapter 7

TAKING RISKS, SEIZING REWARDS

Life is full of opportunities, some planned and others unexpected. To seize these opportunities requires a mindset rooted in the present moment, an embrace of spontaneity, and the courage to take calculated risks. Imagine that you're walking through a bustling street on a tiring day after work. The sun is shining, casting a golden hue over everything, and the air is filled with the sounds of the city – laughter, conversations, music, and the distant hum of traffic. Suddenly, you spot an impromptu street performance by a talented musician. The crowd gathers, mesmerised by the melody. You have a choice: you could walk by, sticking to your plan for the day, or you could seize this unexpected opportunity to experience something beautiful. This chapter is about choosing the latter – embracing the spontaneity of life and making the most of every moment. This is the Carpe Diem mentality.

Living in the moment, or mindfulness, is about fully engaging with the present. It means putting aside distractions and immersing yourself in the current experience. It's the thrill of feeling the wind against your face during a morning jog, the joy of a child's laughter, or the comfort of a heartfelt conversation with a friend.

Why is this important? Because life unfolds in the present. When we're constantly fixated on past regrets or future anxieties, we miss out on the richness of the now. Embracing spontaneity and living in the moment can enhance our experiences, making them more vivid and memorable.

Even I wasn't always the best at this; like any life lesson, this is also something that I learned to nurture and grow over time. On one sunny morning, during my usual walk, I decided to wander a bit off my regular path. The crowded streets and bustling noise had become routine, and I was yearning for something different. That's when I stumbled upon the Bombay Port Trust Park. I had always walked past it but never gave myself the chance to explore. As soon as I entered, I was amazed at how well-maintained and serene it was. It was like stepping into a whole new world – quiet, peaceful, and the perfect spot to unwind and let my thoughts wander. I even got to speak with some elderly folks, around 80-85 years old, who were doing yoga. Their stories and wisdom were incredibly fulfilling. This little sanctuary has now become a cherished part of my morning routine, all thanks to that one spontaneous decision. It's a good reminder to stay present, as you never know what hidden gems you might find.

Living in the moment is not about abandoning responsibility but about appreciating and engaging with life as it happens. It means being aware of your surroundings, your feelings, and your interactions. It's about savouring your morning coffee, genuinely listening during conversations, and feeling the satisfaction of completing a task. This mindset can improve your mental health, reduce stress, and increase overall happiness.

Seizing Unexpected Opportunities

Opportunities often come knocking when least expected, and the ability to recognise and seize them is a hallmark of the Carpe Diem mentality. This doesn't mean you should act recklessly but rather stay open and adaptable to new possibilities.

Consider the story of one of my ex-students, Rehaan; a software developer. Despite his expertise and experience, he felt stagnant in his current role and longed for a fresh challenge. It was during this period of introspection that he decided to attend a tech conference in the hopes of gaining new insights and networking opportunities. As he poured himself a cup of coffee, Rehaan noticed a fellow attendee standing nearby, engrossed in his smartphone. Seizing the opportunity to strike up a conversation, Rehaan introduced himself and initiated a casual chat. The two quickly bonded over their shared interest in emerging technologies and exchanged insights on the latest industry trends.

It was during this conversation that Rehaan's companion, a seasoned entrepreneur attending the conference, shared some invaluable advice. He spoke passionately about the dynamic culture and exciting projects at his startup, emphasising the company's commitment to innovation and growth. Impressed by Rehaan's knowledge and enthusiasm, he extended an invitation for Rehaan to visit their office and learn more about potential opportunities. Thrilled by the unexpected turn of events, Rehaan eagerly accepted the offer and arranged to meet with the entrepreneur later that week. The visit exceeded his expectations, as he was introduced to the talented team behind the startup and given a glimpse into their groundbreaking projects. Inspired by their vision and impressed by Rehaan's skills, the entrepreneur wasted no time in offering him a position on their team. For Rehaan, this spontaneous encounter marked the beginning of an exciting new chapter in his career. By stepping out of his comfort zone and seizing the opportunity to connect with a fellow conference attendee, he had unlocked doors that he never knew existed. The advice he received and the subsequent job offer not only validated his expertise but also reignited his passion for software development.

Looking back, Rehaan couldn't help but marvel at the serendipitous nature of it all. If he had remained closed off or stuck to his original agenda, he would have missed out on the chance to explore new possibilities and embark on a transformative journey. As he embraced the unknown and the Carpe Diem mentality, Rehaan discovered that sometimes, the greatest opportunities lie in the most unexpected places.

"In the midst of the ordinary lies the extraordinary. Sometimes, all it takes is a simple cup of coffee and a conversation to open doors you never knew existed." - Rehaan

Seizing opportunities requires a combination of awareness and readiness. Here are a few strategies:

1. Stay Curious: Always be on the lookout for new experiences and knowledge. Curiosity opens doors to opportunities you might otherwise overlook.
2. Network: Build and maintain relationships. Sometimes, opportunities come through connections and casual conversations.
3. Be Proactive: Don't wait for opportunities to find you. Seek them out, whether it's through attending events, taking up new hobbies, or exploring new career paths.
4. Take Action: When an opportunity presents itself, evaluate it quickly and, if it aligns with your goals and values, act on it. Hesitation can sometimes mean missed chances.

Balancing Adventure with Responsibility

Taking risks is an inherent part of seizing opportunities. However, the key lies in balancing adventure with responsibility. Calculated risks involve thorough evaluation and planning, distinguishing them from reckless gambles.

Embarking on a new venture or making a significant life change can be daunting. It's natural to feel a mix of excitement and trepidation. The thrill of venturing into the unknown is often tempered by the fear of potential failure. This is where the importance of calculated risks comes into play. Taking a calculated risk means you are not just leaping into the dark; instead, you are carefully considering the variables and planning your steps meticulously.

The first step in taking a calculated risk is conducting thorough research. Information is power. Before making any significant decision, gather as much information as possible about the potential risk. Understand the market dynamics, identify the challenges you might face, and evaluate the potential rewards. For instance, if you're considering starting a business, study the industry trends, analyse your competitors, and understand your target audience. This comprehensive research provides a solid foundation for making informed decisions and reduces the element of uncertainty.

Once you have gathered all the necessary information, the next step is to plan ahead. A well-thought-out plan acts as a roadmap, guiding you through the process and helping you stay focused on your goals. Develop a clear plan that outlines your objectives, the steps needed to achieve them, and potential contingency plans for unforeseen challenges. For example, if you plan to transition to a new career, map out the skills you need to acquire, the resources required, and the timeline for achieving your milestones. Planning ahead not only mitigates risks but also prepares you for potential obstacles, enabling you to face them effectively.

Starting small is another crucial aspect of taking calculated risks. Diving headfirst into a new venture without testing the waters can be overwhelming and risky. Instead, consider starting small and gradually scaling up. For instance, if you're passionate about launching a startup, consider beginning with a side hustle while maintaining your current job. This approach allows you to test your business model, gain initial traction, and understand the market response without jeopardising your financial stability. By starting small, you can make adjustments and improvements before fully committing, thereby reducing the risk of significant losses.

Assessing the worst-case scenario is an essential part of the decision-making process. It's important to understand what you stand to lose and decide if you can live with that outcome. This involves a realistic evaluation of the potential downsides and their impact on your life. For example, if you're considering investing a substantial amount of money in that new venture, evaluate the financial implications if the venture fails. Understanding the worst-case scenario helps you make informed decisions and prepares you mentally and financially for possible setbacks. It's about balancing optimism with realism, ensuring that you are prepared for both success and failure.

Trusting your instincts is also crucial when taking calculated risks. While data and planning are critical, sometimes your gut feeling can provide valuable insights. Intuition is often based on a combination of experience, knowledge, and subconscious processing of information. When you've done your homework and thoroughly evaluated the risks, listening to your instincts can guide you in the right direction. For instance, if you've meticulously planned the business venture and all the data points to its viability, but something feels off, it's worth considering your intuition. Trusting your instincts, especially when backed by solid research and planning, can help you make decisions that align with your inner wisdom and values.

In balancing adventure with responsibility, the goal is to pursue your passions and ambitions without recklessly jeopardising your stability. It's about finding the sweet spot where you can embrace the thrill of new opportunities while ensuring that you have a safety net to fall back on. By conducting thorough research, planning ahead, starting small, assessing the worst-case scenario, and trusting your instincts, you can take calculated risks that lead to personal and professional growth. This balanced approach empowers you to seize opportunities confidently, knowing that you have carefully considered and prepared for the journey ahead.

Learning from Failure and Rejection

Failure and rejection are inevitable parts of life, especially when you take risks. However, they are not the end but rather stepping stones to success. Learning to cope with and grow from these experiences is crucial for personal and professional development.

The first step in learning from failure and rejection is reflection. When a project doesn't go as planned or a goal isn't met, it's essential to take a step back and reflect on the experience. This means analysing the situation objectively, without letting emotions cloud your judgement. What were the factors that contributed to the failure? Were there any warning signs that were missed? Reflection helps you identify mistakes and areas for improvement. By understanding the root causes, you can develop a clearer picture of what went wrong and why.

In addition to self-reflection, seeking feedback is an invaluable part of the learning process. Constructive criticism provides perspectives that you might have overlooked. Engaging with colleagues, mentors, or even friends to gather their insights can offer a broader view of the situation. They might point out specific areas where you can improve or suggest alternative approaches that could work better in the future. By being open to feedback, you demonstrate a willingness to learn and grow, which is essential for personal and professional development. It's important to remember that feedback is not a critique of your character but rather an opportunity to enhance your skills and performance.

Maintaining a positive mindset in the face of failure and rejection is also crucial. It's easy to become discouraged and let negativity take over, but focusing on the lessons learned can help you move forward with renewed energy and determination. Instead of dwelling on what went wrong, shift your focus to what you can do better next time. A positive outlook transforms failures into valuable learning experiences, making you more resilient and adaptable. This perspective allows you to see failure as a temporary setback rather than a permanent defeat.

Once you have reflected and gathered feedback, the next step is to adjust and adapt your strategies and approaches. Flexibility is key to overcoming setbacks and achieving long-term success. This might mean revising your plans, adopting new techniques, or changing your mindset. For instance, if a business venture didn't succeed, use the insights gained to refine your business model, improve your marketing strategy, or enhance your product. Adapting to change and being willing to pivot, when necessary, can significantly increase your chances of success in future endeavours. Many successful people faced numerous rejections and failures before achieving their goals. The difference between those who succeed and those who don't often lies in this ability to be flexible and persistent. It's about continuing to push forward, even when the going gets tough. Each failure brings you one step closer to success, as long as you learn from the experience and keep trying. Persistence builds resilience, helping you to withstand future challenges with greater ease.

Thriving in Dynamic Environments

In today's fast-paced and ever-changing world, the ability to thrive in dynamic environments is a crucial skill. Whether it's adapting to new technologies, changing market conditions, or evolving job roles, those who can embrace and flourish amidst change will find greater success and satisfaction. As we traverse the complexities of modern life, it becomes increasingly important to develop strategies and mindsets that enable us to not just cope with change but to leverage it for our growth and benefit.

One of the foundational aspects of thriving in dynamic environments is staying informed. In a rapidly evolving landscape, information is power. Keeping up with industry trends, technological advancements, and market changes is essential. This doesn't mean you need to become an expert in every new development, but having a broad awareness of what is happening in your field and related areas can provide a significant advantage. Regularly reading industry publications, attending webinars, and participating in professional networks can help you stay ahead of the curve. By anticipating shifts and trends, you can position yourself to take advantage of new opportunities and avoid being blindsided by sudden changes.

However, staying informed is only the first step. The next crucial element is committing to continuous learning. In a dynamic environment, the skills and knowledge that were relevant yesterday might not be sufficient tomorrow. Embracing lifelong learning means continuously updating your skills and expanding your knowledge base. This could involve taking formal courses, attending workshops, or engaging in self-directed learning through books, online resources, and practical experience. The willingness to learn and adapt is what separates those who thrive from those who merely survive. By making learning a habit, you ensure that you remain adaptable and competitive in an ever-changing world.

Being proactive is another key to thriving in dynamic environments. Rather than waiting for change to happen and reacting to it, seek out new opportunities and be willing to innovate and experiment. This proactive approach involves taking calculated risks and stepping out of your comfort zone. For instance, if you notice a new technology emerging in your industry, take the initiative to learn about it and explore how it could be applied in your work. Being proactive also means staying open to new ideas and approaches, even if they challenge the status quo. By taking the initiative, you demonstrate leadership and a forward-thinking mindset that can set you apart from your peers.

In addition to being proactive, embracing diversity is essential for thriving in dynamic environments. Diverse perspectives can provide valuable insights and solutions that might not be apparent from a single viewpoint. This diversity can come from a variety of sources, including team members with different backgrounds, experiences, and areas of expertise. By fostering an inclusive environment that values diverse contributions, you can enhance creativity and innovation. Encouraging open dialogue and collaboration among team members can lead to more effective problem-solving and better decision-making. Embracing diversity also means being open to new ways of thinking and being willing to learn from others, regardless of their background or position.

In the digital age, thriving in dynamic environments also involves leveraging technology to your advantage. The rapid pace of technological change means that new tools and platforms are constantly emerging, offering new ways to work, communicate, and innovate. Staying current with digital trends and incorporating new technologies into your workflow can enhance your productivity and effectiveness. For example, using project management software can streamline collaboration and keep projects on track, while data analytics tools can provide insights that inform better decision-making. Being comfortable with technology and willing to experiment with new tools can give you a competitive edge in a rapidly changing landscape.

Moreover, digital literacy goes beyond just using new tools; it involves understanding the broader implications of digital transformation. This includes being aware of issues such as data privacy, cybersecurity, and the ethical use of technology. As more aspects of work and life become digitised, being knowledgeable about these areas becomes increasingly important. Staying informed about digital trends and best practices can help you make informed decisions.

Another aspect of thriving in dynamic environments is the ability to manage stress and maintain wellbeing. Rapid changes and uncertainty can be sources of stress, but developing effective coping mechanisms can help you stay resilient and focused. This might involve practices such as mindfulness, exercise, and maintaining a healthy work-life balance. Mindfulness techniques, such as meditation and deep breathing, can help you stay grounded and centred, even in the midst of change. Regular physical activity can reduce stress and improve overall wellbeing, while a balanced approach to work and personal life ensures that you have the energy and perspective to handle challenges effectively.

Seizing opportunities through a Carpe Diem mentality involves a delicate balance of living in the moment, taking calculated risks, and thriving amidst change and uncertainty. By embracing spontaneity and staying open to unexpected opportunities, you allow yourself to experience the richness of life's possibilities. Building resilience enables you to turn life's setbacks into stepping stones for success.

Remember, the journey is just as important as the destination. Each moment holds the potential for growth and discovery. Embrace each moment with mindfulness, take bold steps with thoughtful preparation, and continuously learn and grow. Life is a grand adventure waiting to be explored. By adopting the Carpe Diem mentality, you can seize life with both hands and live fully, finding joy and fulfilment in every step of your journey. Embrace the present, embrace the change, and most importantly, embrace yourself.

Key Learnings:

1. Embracing the present moment, or mindfulness, allows us to fully engage with our experiences, enhancing their richness and vividness. By putting aside distractions and immersing ourselves in the now, we can reduce stress, improve mental health, and increase overall happiness.

2. Opportunities often arise when least expected, and the ability to recognise and seize them is vital for personal and professional growth. Staying curious, building networks, being proactive, and taking decisive action are key strategies for seizing unexpected opportunities and capitalising on them.

3. Taking risks is inherent in seizing opportunities, but it's essential to balance adventure with responsibility. Calculated risks involve thorough research, strategic planning, starting small, assessing worst-case scenarios, and trusting instincts. By striking this balance, we can pursue our passions while minimising potential downsides.

4. The ability to thrive in dynamic environments is crucial. Staying informed, committing to continuous learning, being proactive, embracing diversity, leveraging technology, managing stress, and maintaining wellbeing are essential strategies for thriving amidst change and uncertainty.

Action Items:

1. Identify a goal or opportunity that excites you, which might involve some level of risk. Conduct thorough research, develop a plan, start small, assess potential

outcomes, and trust your instincts. Take decisive action and be prepared to adjust course as needed.

2. Reflect on past failures or rejections and identify lessons learned. Seek feedback from trusted mentors or peers, maintain a positive mindset, and use insights gained to adjust your strategies and approaches. Remember that failure is not a reflection of your worth but a stepping stone to success.

3. Dedicate time each week to staying informed about industry trends, technological advancements, and market changes. Commit to continuous learning through online courses, workshops, or self-directed study. Be proactive in adapting to new challenges and opportunities that arise.

Chapter 8

YOUR NORTH STAR

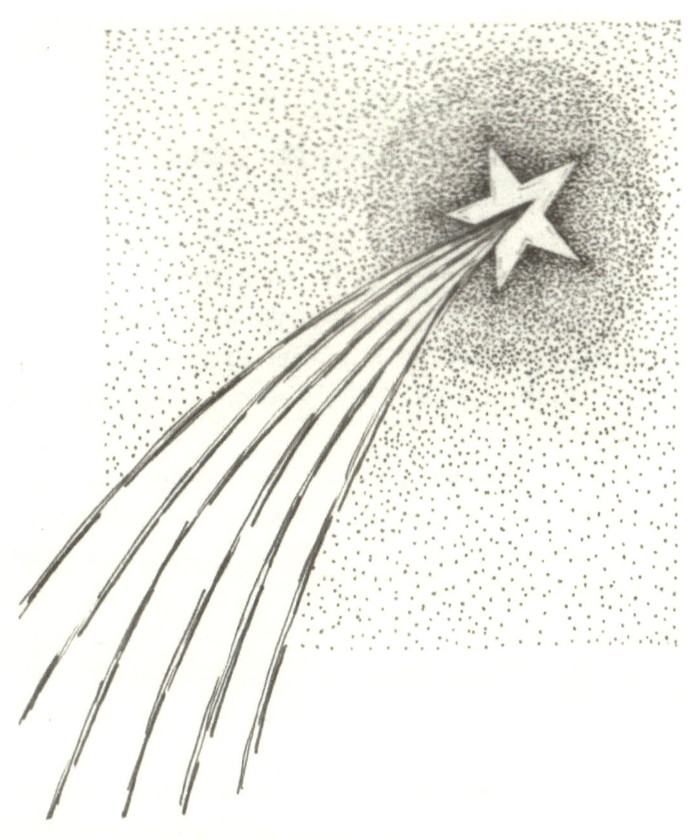

In the journey of self-discovery and personal growth, understanding your values and passions, as discussed in Chapter 1, forms the foundation for creating a meaningful and fulfilling life. Knowing what truly matters to you and what ignites your enthusiasm provides the clarity needed to mitigate the obstacles of life. With this understanding in place, you can now focus on the next crucial step: creating a personal mission statement. A mission statement encapsulates your purpose, values, and aspirations, serving as a compass to steer your life towards your true north.

Creating a Personal Purpose Declaration

A Personal Purpose Declaration is a concise declaration of your purpose and the guiding principles that shape your life. It serves as a roadmap for your journey, providing clarity and focus in decision-making and goal-setting. Crafting a declaration statement involves thoughtful consideration of your values, passions, and long-term aspirations.

Begin by defining your purpose. Your purpose is the overarching reason that drives your life. It reflects your deepest motivations and the impact you want to make in the world. To define your purpose, consider what you want to be remembered for, how you want to contribute to the lives of others, and the legacy you want to leave behind. Your purpose should be inspiring and reflect your highest aspirations.

Articulate your values in your declaration statement. As discussed earlier, your values are the principles that are most important to you and guide your decisions and actions. Reflect on the values you identified earlier and think about how they influence your life. Ensure that your statement aligns with these values and serves as a constant reminder of what you stand for. Incorporate your passions into your declaration by considering how they contribute to your sense of fulfilment and purpose. Think about the activities that bring you the greatest joy and how they can be integrated into your daily life. Your declaration should reflect your commitment to pursuing these passions and leveraging them to achieve your goals.

Remember to keep your Personal Purpose Declaration concise. It should be clear, easy to remember, and capture the essence of your purpose, values, and passions. Avoid overly complex language or vague statements. Instead, focus on creating a statement that is both inspiring and actionable.

For example, a Personal Purpose Declaration might read: "As a paediatric nurse, I am dedicated to providing compassionate and high-quality care to children, fostering a supportive and comforting environment for both patients and their families. Through continuous learning and professional development, I strive to stay at the forefront of paediatric care, inspiring my colleagues with my commitment to excellence and empathy."

Another example could be: "As a parent, I aim to create a nurturing and stimulating home environment where my children feel loved, respected, and encouraged to pursue their interests and dreams. By actively participating in their education and personal development, I hope to instil in them values of kindness, curiosity, and resilience, guiding them to become confident and compassionate individuals."

These statements are specific, reflect core values and passions, and provide clear direction for the individual's professional and personal life.

Visualising Your Ideal Future

Visualisation is a powerful tool for achieving your goals and staying motivated on your journey. By creating a vivid mental image of your ideal future, you can strengthen your commitment to your vision and increase your confidence in your ability to achieve it. By acquiring new skills, pursuing further studies, and building my confidence, I began to see the fruits of my hard work. People started to notice my efforts, and my career trajectory took a significant leap. I went from being unsure about my career to the Head of School, but it didn't happen overnight. It took years of tweaking the formula until I knew what was right for me.

It was during this upward journey that I began to dare to dream bigger and also encountered the concept of vision boards. I approached it with a mix of curiosity and scepticism, but I ended up realising that there was nothing to lose. Slowly but surely, many of the things that I put up on my vision board started to come true, and changing it up every 3-4 months also gave me a tangible space to review my goals from time to time. Among these goals were authoring a book and studying at the Indian Institute of Management Ahmedabad (IIMA), both of which have come to fruition. Creating a vision board became a transformative practice for me. It serves as a visual representation of my goals and aspirations, encapsulating the images, words, and symbols that resonate with my vision and inspire me. I gather materials such as magazines, photos, and art supplies and create a collage that reflects my ideal future. This vision board occupies a prominent location in my bedroom above my desk, where I see it daily, constantly reminding me of my goals and keeping my motivation alive.

Journaling is another powerful visualisation tool I use to manifest my goals. Each day, I take time to write about my goals and dreams in a journal. This practice allows me to articulate my vision in words, making it more concrete and tangible. I describe my ideal future in detail, including the emotions I will feel, the actions I will take, and the people I will interact with. By writing these things down, I reinforce my belief in my ability to achieve them. Journaling also helps me track my progress and reflect on my journey. I can see how far I've come and what steps I need to take next. It's a way to stay accountable and focused. According to a 2021 survey by the Indian Journal of Psychiatry, journaling is becoming a popular therapeutic tool among young Indians, with 45% of respondents between the ages of 18-30 reporting that they journal regularly to manage stress and anxiety. When I look back at past entries, I can see the growth and changes in my thoughts and goals, which motivates me to keep moving forward.

Praying is a deeply personal and spiritual aspect of my visualisation practice. It's a way for me to connect with a higher power and seek guidance and strength on my journey. Through prayer, I express my hopes, dreams, and fears, and ask for support in achieving my goals. Praying helps me stay grounded and centred, reminding me that I am not alone on this journey. I pray daily, often incorporating affirmations into my prayers. I say things like, "I am capable of achieving my goals and living my best life," and "I am committed to pursuing my passions and making a positive impact on the world." These affirmations boost my confidence and keep me aligned with my path. Prayer also provides a sense of peace and reassurance. It's a reminder that, even when things get tough, there is a higher power guiding and supporting me. This belief gives me the strength to persevere and stay committed to my vision.

Together, these tools of visualisation—vision boards, journaling, and praying—form a comprehensive practice that keeps me focused, motivated, and inspired. Each tool complements the others, creating a holistic approach to manifesting my goals. The vision board provides a visual representation of my dreams, making them tangible and real. Journaling allows me to articulate and track my progress, keeping me accountable and reflective. Praying offers spiritual support and reassurance, reminding me of the higher power guiding my journey.

Through this process, I've learned that visualisation is not just about imagining a better future but actively creating it. The power of visualisation lies in its ability to transform abstract dreams into tangible goals and actionable plans. My journey from scepticism to belief in visualisation is a testament to this transformative power. Visualisation, combined with hard work and perseverance, enables me to achieve goals I once thought were beyond my reach.

As you embark on your journey of visualising your ideal future, remember that the practice is deeply personal and unique to each individual. Create a vision board that speaks to your aspirations, practise daily journaling to articulate your goals, and use prayer to seek guidance and support. Embrace the process with an open heart and a positive mindset, and watch as your dreams begin to take shape and become reality.

Overcoming Distractions and Detours

Creating a vision board and visualising your dreams can be exhilarating and inspiring. However, staying on track and consistently working towards your goals can be challenging. It's easy to get distracted or lose focus, and these distractions can quickly derail your progress. By saying there is no room for errors, we are creating errors. It's essential to acknowledge that setbacks and distractions are part of the journey, but they don't have to define it. In this section, we'll explore how to avoid distractions, stay committed to your path, and ensure that your vision boards and other visualisation tools remain effective.

Identifying Potential Distractions

Distractions are everywhere. From the constant ping of social media notifications to the lure of binge-watching TV shows, there are countless ways to lose focus. To stay committed to your goals, it's crucial to identify the distractions that are most likely to affect you.

One of the biggest distractions is social media. While it can be a great tool for staying connected and inspired, it can also consume a significant amount of time. I've seen this firsthand with one of my daughter's friends, Neel. He's an incredibly talented graphic designer with big dreams of starting his own design studio. However, he found himself spending hours scrolling through Instagram and Facebook each day. Despite his talent and ambition, his progress was slow because he wasn't dedicating enough time to his goals.

Another common distraction is excessive screen time, whether it's watching TV, playing video games, or aimlessly browsing the internet. My colleague, Anahita, used to spend her evenings aimlessly binge-watching one show after the other, especially after a long day at work. She had dreams of running a marathon but never seemed to find the time to train. By the end of the day, she felt too tired to go for a run, and her training plan often fell by the wayside.

Identifying these distractions is the first step towards minimising their impact. Reflect on your daily routines and habits to pinpoint where you might be losing time or focus.

Setting Boundaries

Once you've identified potential distractions, the next step is to set clear boundaries to protect your time and energy. Establishing boundaries is essential to staying focused and making consistent progress towards your goals.

For example, Neel decided to set specific times for checking social media. He allocated time in the morning and evening to check social media, and during the rest of the day, he turned off notifications while working and kept his phone out of reach. This simple change allowed him to dedicate more time to his design projects, and he started to see significant progress.

Anahita also made changes to her routine. She set a boundary of watching much less TV. This freed up time for her to train for her marathon. She also found that the physical activity helped her relax and sleep better, which improved her overall productivity.

Creating a dedicated workspace can also help set boundaries. When you have a specific area designated for working on your goals, it becomes easier to focus and avoid distractions. Whether it's a home office, a corner of your living room, or a spot at a local café, having a space where you can concentrate on your tasks is invaluable. In my case, everyone in my home knows that the desk in my room is sacrosanct; when I'm sitting at it, I don't entertain any interruptions, and it puts me in a space of discipline; a place where I can truly disconnect from my distractions and get to work!

Communicating your boundaries to others is very important. Let your family and friends know about your goals and the boundaries you've set to achieve them. Ask for their support in respecting your time and space. Most people will be more than willing to help you stay on track once they understand your commitment and the importance of your goals.

Staying Organised

Organisation is key to maintaining focus and staying committed to your path. When you're organised, you can manage your time effectively and avoid feeling overwhelmed by your goals.

One way to stay organised is by using tools and techniques such as to-do lists, planners, and digital calendars. These tools can help you keep track of your tasks and deadlines, ensuring that you stay on top of your commitments. For instance, my friend Manisha, a writer, found herself constantly juggling multiple projects and deadlines. She started using a timeboxing planner to organise her tasks and set reminders for important milestones. This helped her prioritise her work and stay focused on her goals. As a result, she was able to complete her projects on time and even take on new opportunities that aligned with her long-term vision.

Creating a daily or weekly schedule can also help you stay organised. Allocate specific times for working on your goals and stick to this schedule as much as possible. By treating these blocks of time as non-negotiable appointments, you can ensure that you make consistent progress.

Embracing Imperfections

One of the biggest obstacles to staying committed to your path is the fear of making mistakes. By saying there is no room for errors, we are creating errors. It's important to recognise that mistakes and setbacks are a natural part of the journey. Embracing imperfections and learning from them can help you stay focused and resilient.

I remember a time when I was working on my book and hit a major writer's block. I started to doubt myself and my ability to complete the project. I felt like every sentence I wrote was a mistake, and this fear of imperfection paralysed me. It was then that I reminded myself that progress is more important than perfection. I allowed myself to write imperfectly, knowing that I could always revise and improve my work later. This shift in mindset helped me break through the block and eventually complete my book.

Ultimately, the effectiveness of your vision boards, journaling, and other visualisation tools depends on your ability to stay focused and avoid distractions. Only you are in the way of your progress. Holding yourself accountable is crucial to staying committed to your goals. Regularly review your vision board and journal entries to remind yourself of your goals and the progress you've made. Set specific, measurable goals and track your progress. If you find yourself getting off track, don't be too hard on yourself. Acknowledge the setback, learn from it, and refocus on your path. Having an accountability partner can also be incredibly helpful. Find someone who shares your commitment to personal growth and check in with each other regularly. Share your goals, progress, and challenges, and support each other in staying on track. By fostering a sense of responsibility and collaboration, accountability partners can be instrumental in helping individuals maintain their dedication to their goals.

Key Learnings:

1. A personal mission statement encapsulates your purpose, values, and aspirations, offering clarity and focus in decision-making.
2. Visualisation, through vision boards, journaling, and praying, can transform abstract dreams into tangible goals and actionable plans.
3. Recognising and managing distractions is crucial for maintaining focus and ensuring consistent progress towards your goals.
4. Accepting mistakes as part of the journey allows for growth and resilience, preventing the fear of failure from hindering progress.

Action Items:

1. Create a concise mission statement that captures your purpose, values, and passions. Ensure it is inspiring and actionable.
2. Dedicate time each day to write about your goals, dreams, and progress. Use journaling to articulate your vision, track your journey, and stay accountable.
3. Communicate your goals and boundaries to family and friends. Have dinner table conversations. Create a dedicated workspace and establish non-negotiable times for working on your goals.
4. Identify someone who shares your commitment to personal growth. Schedule regular check-ins to discuss goals, progress, and challenges and support each other in staying on track.

Chapter 9

3HS - HEAD, HEART AND HAND

On the journey of self-discovery and personal growth, it's crucial to remember that true success isn't solely about personal achievement or career milestones. It's also about the impact we have on others and the world around us. Cultivating kindness and compassion, both towards ourselves and others, forms the foundation of a fulfilling and meaningful life. This chapter will explore how practising random acts of kindness, developing empathy, and fostering gratitude can help us stay grounded and connected, even as we strive to reach our goals. By engaging our heads, hearts, and hands, we can create a ripple effect of positivity and make a significant difference in the lives of those around us. The concept of the "3H's: Head, Heart, and Hand," explores the significance of practising kindness and compassion in all aspects of your life. The "Head" represents understanding and empathy, the "Heart" symbolises love and compassion, and the "Hand" signifies action and service. Together, these elements form the foundation of a life grounded in kindness and compassion.

Head: Intellectual Understanding

The head represents the intellectual aspect of kindness and compassion. It involves understanding different perspectives, recognising life's blessings, and making a conscious effort to practise gratitude and empathy.

Heart: Emotional Connection

The heart symbolises the emotional connection to kindness and compassion. It involves feeling empathy for others, connecting on a deeper level, and finding joy in everyday moments. This emotional connection enriches your relationships and fosters a sense of love and compassion in your interactions.

Hand: Taking Action

The hand signifies the practical application of kindness and compassion. It involves performing acts of kindness, making a difference in others' lives, and taking concrete steps to support and uplift those around you. This action-oriented approach brings your intellectual understanding and emotional connection to life, creating a tangible impact on the world.

You can incorporate the 3Hs in your daily life by practising sweet and simple acts of gratitude. It is a powerful way to spread positivity and joy. These acts can be as simple as a smile to a stranger, holding the door open for someone, or buying a coffee for the person in line behind you. Such small gestures, though seemingly insignificant, can have a profound impact on someone's day.

One of the most beautiful aspects of kindness is its contagious nature. When you perform an act of kindness, it often inspires others to do the same. This ripple effect can create a wave of positivity that spreads far beyond your immediate circle. For example, imagine you're in a crowded grocery store, and you notice a cashier looking stressed. You take a moment to compliment their efficiency and thank them for their hard work. This simple act of recognition can lift their spirits, improve their mood, and potentially lead them to treat the next customer with more patience and warmth. Spreading positivity doesn't always require grand gestures. It can be as simple as leaving a kind note for a coworker, sending an encouraging message to a friend, or volunteering a few hours of your time to a local charity. These small acts of kindness accumulate, creating an environment of goodwill and compassion.

Developing Empathy

Empathy, the ability to understand and share the feelings of others, is crucial for building deeper connections and fostering a compassionate society.

Empathy starts with the head, requiring us to step outside our own experiences and consider the viewpoints of others. This can be challenging, especially when those perspectives differ significantly from our own. However, by engaging with diverse groups of people and exposing ourselves to different cultures and experiences, we can broaden our understanding.

For example, participate in cultural festivals, community events, or join organisations that bring together people from various backgrounds. Reading books, watching documentaries, and consuming media that represent different perspectives can also expand your worldview. It can even be as simple as talking to people you generally wouldn't have conversations with. It could be your barber, at the salon, or the barista at your neighbourhood café. Simply engaging in conversations with people from different walks of life will help you appreciate the richness of the experiences and perspectives that exist around you.

Empathy also involves the heart—feeling what others feel. This emotional connection can transform relationships and interactions. To truly connect with others, practice active listening. Pay attention not just to the words being spoken but also to the emotions behind them. Show genuine interest in their experiences and express empathy by acknowledging their feelings.

Consider the story of Ananya, one of my ex-students who interned with an NGO in her first year of college, working with underprivileged children. Ananya's first day at the NGO was eye-opening. The children she met came from families struggling to make ends meet, living in cramped quarters with limited access to basic amenities. She couldn't help but feel a pang of shock and guilt as she contrasted their living conditions with her own comfortable upbringing, and even the fact that to her, this was just another developmental internship. As she spent more time with the children, Ananya began to see beyond their immediate circumstances. She listened intently to their stories—of dreams to become doctors, teachers, and even artists. She saw their faces light up when they talked about their favourite subjects in school or shared their ambitions for the future. Despite the challenges they faced, these children exuded resilience and optimism. Ananya learned not only about their dreams but also about the daily hurdles they faced: from a lack of educational resources to financial instability at home. She heard about their struggles with peer pressure and their hopes for a brighter tomorrow. These conversations were a stark reminder of the systemic inequalities that shaped their lives but also of the strength and determination within each child.

Empathy must translate into action. The most natural next step should be to take steps to support and uplift them. This could involve advocating for social causes, participating in community service, or simply being there for someone in need. In fact, even when it comes to a professional setting, a 2023 survey by the Indian Institute of Management (IIM) Ahmedabad highlighted that empathy in leadership is becoming increasingly important in Indian workplaces. The study found that 65% of Indian employees valued empathetic leadership and believed it led to better team collaboration and higher job satisfaction. The experience at the NGO became a turning point for Ananya. It ignited a passion within her to make a tangible difference in the lives of these children and others facing similar challenges. She became actively involved in organising educational workshops, mentoring sessions, and fundraising events to support their aspirations. Ananya's commitment to social justice and equity grew stronger as she continued to advocate for resources and opportunities for underprivileged youth. Her journey illustrates how direct engagement with communities can transform one's perspective and deepen empathy. It teaches us that empathy involves not only seeing and hearing but also actively listening, understanding, and taking meaningful action to create positive change.

Fostering Gratitude

Gratitude is the practice of recognising and appreciating the positive aspects of life. It shifts our focus from what we lack to what we have, fostering contentment and joy. This practice can be truly transformative, enriching our lives and enhancing our relationships. Let's dive into how we can foster gratitude using the combined power of our head, heart, and hand.

Gratitude starts with the heart—a genuine emotional response to the goodness in our lives. It's about feeling a deep sense of appreciation for the small and big blessings that come our way. One way to nurture this feeling is by starting a gratitude journal. Each day, write down three things you're grateful for. These can range from significant events, like a promotion at work, to small joys, like a beautiful sunset or a kind word from a friend. This practice helps shift our mental focus from what's missing in our lives to the abundance that surrounds us.

Think about a day when everything seemed to go wrong. Even on such days, finding those little moments of joy can change our perspective. Maybe it's the comfort of a warm cup of chai, the smile of a stranger, or the support of a loved one. Recognising these moments helps us appreciate life's simple pleasures.

While gratitude starts with the heart, it's sustained by the head – a conscious effort to recognise and appreciate the good things in life. This mental shift can profoundly impact our outlook and attitude. Whether it's bullet journaling, timeboxing, or just picking up a notebook and writing what you feel, it's crucial to understand and be grateful for what you have. Many of us love to compartmentalise our tasks to manage our work better, but how many of us like to compartmentalise our emotions and feelings? Let's not take what we've got for granted.

Consider taking a few minutes each day to focus on the positive aspects of your life. Whether it's enjoying a cup of chai, spending time with loved ones, or taking a walk in the park, these moments of mindfulness can enrich your life and deepen your sense of gratitude. This will teach you to be grateful for the seemingly mundane events of the day, like watering the plants with your mother or dropping your sister off at college.

Expressing gratitude through action reinforces its impact. It's one thing to feel grateful, but taking steps to show it can magnify its effect. Thank the people who have made a difference in your life, volunteer your time to give back to the community, and find ways to share your blessings with others. For instance, if you've received support in your career, consider mentoring someone else. In an Indian context, where gratitude is deeply rooted in cultural and familial traditions, actions like participating in community festivals, helping with family responsibilities, or supporting local artisans by buying their products can significantly enhance your practice of gratitude.

Let me share a story about my mentor, my guide, the most respectable, Sir D. Sivanandan, and his inspiring work with the Roti Bank. After his retirement from the state police as Director General of Police (DGP), Sir D. Sivanandan initiated a mission to serve the needy by setting up Maharashtra's first 'Roti Bank' in 2018. The Roti Bank started as a food rescue organisation that collected excess food from hotels and events to be distributed among hungry people. Today, it has its own kitchens designed to feed children nutritious cooked food and snacks in schools and slums, providing 12,000 meals every day.

Working with Sir Sivanandan and the Roti Bank taught me invaluable lessons about gratitude. Seeing the smiles on the faces of children receiving meals, understanding the profound impact of what might seem like a small act of kindness, and realising how interconnected we all are reinforced the importance of giving back. His vision is now expanding across the country, with plans to extend services to various states, ensuring that no one sleeps hungry.

The process of fostering gratitude is most powerful when it involves the head, heart, and hand together. The head helps us recognise and consciously appreciate our blessings. The heart allows us to feel genuine gratitude and joy. The hand translates these feelings into actions that can positively impact others. This holistic approach ensures that gratitude is not just a fleeting emotion but a sustained practice that enriches our lives and the lives of those around us.

Incorporate the 3H's in your daily life. Start by acknowledging your blessings (head), feeling deeply thankful for them (heart), and taking action to express this gratitude (hand). Whether it's helping a neighbour, volunteering at a local charity, or simply being present and supportive for your friends and family, these actions will amplify your sense of gratitude and create a ripple effect of positivity.

Overcoming Selfishness on Your Way Up

As you pursue your personal and professional goals, it's crucial to remain grounded in kindness and compassion. The drive for success can sometimes lead to selfishness, where the focus shifts solely to personal gain at the expense of others. Overcoming this tendency requires a conscious effort to balance ambition with empathy and service.

Ambition and compassion are not mutually exclusive; they can coexist and complement each other. To balance these qualities, ensure that your goals align with your values and the wellbeing of others. For instance, if you're aiming for a promotion at work, consider how your leadership can positively impact your team and organisation. Reflect on your motivations and ask yourself if your pursuit of success is benefiting others as well. By integrating compassion into your ambitions, you can achieve your goals while making a positive difference in the lives of those around you.

Staying grounded in kindness and compassion requires regular self-reflection and mindfulness. Take time to assess your actions and their impact on others. Are you prioritising personal gain over the wellbeing of those around you? Are your actions aligned with your values of kindness and empathy? Regularly check in with yourself and make adjustments as needed to ensure that your actions reflect your commitment to kindness and compassion.

As you climb the ladder of success, remember to support others on their journey. Offer mentorship, guidance, and encouragement to those who are following a similar path. By helping others succeed, you create a culture of support and kindness that benefits everyone. Supporting each other can have a transformative impact. By lifting each other up, we create a more compassionate and inclusive society.

Key Learnings:

1. Integrating intellectual understanding (head), emotional connection (Heart), and practical action (hand) forms a holistic approach to living a life grounded in kindness and compassion.

2. Empathy requires both understanding and feeling the experiences of others. It begins with expanding your worldview and actively listening to different perspectives, ultimately leading to meaningful action that supports others' wellbeing.

3. Gratitude shifts our focus from what we lack to appreciating what we have. It involves recognising life's blessings, finding joy in everyday moments, and expressing appreciation through actions that benefit others.

Action Items:

1. Incorporate small acts of kindness into your daily routine, such as complimenting someone, offering help to a stranger, or volunteering your time for a cause you care about.

2. Start a daily gratitude practice by writing down three things you're thankful for each day. This habit cultivates a positive mindset and encourages you to appreciate the blessings in your life.

3. Translate empathy and gratitude into tangible actions. Get involved in community service, mentorship programmes, or advocacy efforts that align with your values of kindness and compassion.

Chapter 10

BRIDGES NOT WALLS

When I first set foot on the campus of Harvard University, the sense of achievement was almost overwhelming. As I walked through the gates, I felt like I was stepping into a different world – one that was steeped in history, intellect, and innovation. This was the place where some of the greatest minds had walked, and now, I was a part of it. But with that excitement came the realisation that I was also stepping into uncharted territory. I was leaving behind the familiar comforts of home and entering a world where I was a stranger.

The journey to Harvard was not just a physical one; it was a journey that had started long before I boarded the flight to Boston. It was a journey of growth, perseverance, and determination. My path had been shaped by the challenges I had faced, the lessons I had learned, and the people who had guided me along the way. As I packed my bags, I couldn't help but reflect on how far I had come – from a young girl with dreams too big for her circumstances, to a woman ready to take on the world.

From the moment I arrived, I was greeted with warmth and kindness. The faculty at Harvard made me feel welcome, and I was deeply honoured when the Dean of HGSE, Katherine K. Merseth, personally acknowledged my effort to be the first to arrive at Longfellow Hall after a gruelling 16-hour journey. Her words, "Arwa, you must be the first one here," were more than just a comment on my punctuality; they were a validation of my presence, a reminder that I belonged here. It was a small gesture, but it meant the world to me. It set the tone for the months ahead, and I knew that I was in the right place.

However, the excitement of being at Harvard soon gave way to the reality of adjusting to a new culture. As the only Indian among 200 participants from various parts of the world, I often found myself feeling like an outsider. Breakfasts were solitary affairs, and I sometimes felt the weight of being different. But I reminded myself that I was here to learn, to grow, and to challenge myself. Breaking new ground was never easy, and I was determined to make the most of this opportunity.

Embracing the Unknown: Beginnings with Hope

The early days were filled with a sense of anticipation and uncertainty. I arrived early for every session, completed my assignments promptly, and volunteered to help others whenever I could. I knew that I had to prove myself, not just to others, but to myself. Slowly, I began to find my place. I went from being an observer to an active participant, from being a newcomer to a valued member of the team. It wasn't long before I was leading group projects and taking charge of the final presentation.

Building bridges in an environment where you feel like an outsider requires resilience, patience, and an open mind. It's about finding common ground while celebrating differences. It's about challenging stereotypes, not just in others, but in yourself. As the days passed, I began to form connections with my peers. I shared the richness of Indian culture, and in return, I learned from their experiences. By consistently participating and demonstrating my commitment, I was able to shift perceptions and build meaningful relationships.

One of the most profound connections I made was with a fellow participant from Pakistan. In a world often divided by politics and borders, our friendship was a testament to the power of human connection.

We supported each other through the challenges of the programme, and by the end, we had become more than just classmates – we had become friends. Our bond was a reminder that, at the end of the day, we are all more alike than we are different.

Building Bridges: Fostering Inclusive Communities

Creating inclusive communities is about more than just being present; it's about being engaged, being open, and being willing to challenge your own assumptions. My experience at Harvard reinforced the importance of resilience and persistence in breaking down barriers. By remaining open and approachable, I was able to win over those who were initially distant. The same group leader who seemed preoccupied at the beginning became one of my strongest supporters by the end of the programme. We bonded over our shared experiences, and by the time we delivered the final presentation, we were no longer just a group – we were a team.

The final presentation was a moment of immense pride and validation. Standing before 200 people, including the Dean and faculty members, I felt a surge of confidence as I delivered the presentation. The standing ovation from my group was a testament to the bridges we had built together. This experience was a reminder that sometimes, we need to assert our presence with kindness and confidence to make our mark in a new environment.

My time at Harvard was transformative in more ways than one. It taught me the importance of persistence, of pushing through the discomfort, and of always staying true to myself. It also taught me the value of using my privilege to make a difference. Inspired by the lessons I had learned, I returned home with a renewed sense of purpose. I wanted to take the knowledge and experiences I had gained and use them to create positive change.

Back home, I gathered students from my school and extended my efforts to the underprivileged students of NM Joshi Municipal School through a collaboration with the Rotary Club of Bombay and their initiative, Project Bhavishya Yaan (Future Wheel). Recognizing the need for improved spoken English, life skills, and computer skills in vernacular medium schools, we conceptualised Bhavishya Yaan, a programme in partnership with the Rotary Club of Bombay that now thrives in eight BMC schools across Mumbai. I designed and oversaw a curriculum called Life Skills Education 101, encompassing mindfulness, meditation, yoga, nutrition, an entrepreneurial mindset, self-defence, and etiquette. My students, under my guidance, dedicated their post-school hours to teaching these vital life skills.

This initiative culminated in a beautiful felicitation ceremony at The Taj Mahal Palace Hotel, in the presence of experienced business owners and highly qualified educationists, celebrating our collective efforts and the impact we made. Reflecting on this experience, I realised that the lesson I learned at Harvard about the responsibility that comes with privilege had come full circle. Just as I had earned the respect of my peers through persistence and dedication, my students learned to use their advantages to uplift and empower others. The ripple effect that the power of education can cause is truly undeniable, and doing it in a supportive and warm environment makes it an unforgettable experience. Humanity, empathy, and the power of giving back are values that extend far beyond the classroom; they actually make a tangible impact in the lives of others, especially those less fortunate.

As I reflect on my journey at Harvard, I am filled with a sense of gratitude. Gratitude for the experiences, for the people I met, and for the lessons I learned. It was a journey of growth, of challenges, and of triumphs. It was a journey that taught me the value of resilience, of persistence, and of the power of human connection. Most importantly, it was a journey that reinforced my belief in the importance of building bridges, not walls.

Key Learnings

1. Persistence always pays off, and coupled with confidence, it can turn any situation around.
2. In difficult situations, we have the choice to either seek comfort or challenge ourselves to grow. Choosing the latter often leads to greater strength and resilience.
3. Sometimes, people may be unaware of the impact of their behaviour. By sharing our unique perspectives, we can help foster understanding and break down barriers.
4. Standing up for others' rights and using our privilege to effect positive change can create a more just and inclusive society.

Action Items

1. Change doesn't have to be great. It can also be tiny. So, find out the closest areas in your life where you can see indifference and inequality, and try to apply a small positive step to change that. You can't change the system, but you can definitely be a positive part of it.
2. Be an ally and advocate for those who are marginalised or discriminated against. It can be someone in your classroom, someone at work, or even someone at home. Use your voice and privilege to support positive change.
3. Find ways to contribute to your community. Volunteer your time, support local initiatives, and make a positive impact. Giving back is not reserved for the rich.

4. Believe in yourself, always participate. What's the worst that could happen?

5. Confidence does not happen overnight. Be mindful of connections, dressing, knowledge, networking, and above all, smiling with grace throughout your journey.

Chapter 11

MENTAL GYM, ONE REP AT A TIME!

Mental health is an essential yet often overlooked aspect of overall wellbeing. Many of us can be too fixated on our external appearance, assuming that if we look good, we must be feeling good as well. However, our mental state isn't always reflected in how we appear on the outside. You've likely heard the term 'mental health' enough times to understand its basic meaning, but knowing what it is doesn't necessarily equate to cultivating good mental health. Mental health is much more than just the mood you're in; it encompasses our emotional, psychological, and social wellbeing. This affects everything from how we think, feel, and act to our ability to handle stress, relate to others, and make important decisions.

When life gets busy, it's easy to overlook these aspects, which is why mental health problems are so prevalent. According to the World Health Organisation (WHO), one in four people will experience mental health issues at some point in their lives. Given the social stigma and lack of awareness surrounding mental health, the actual number might be even higher. That's why it's crucial to recognise the signs of mental health issues and seek help when needed.

There was a time when I was the life of the party. I was known among my family and friends as a jovial clown, someone who always found joy in the tiniest of things. Our youth can be filled with such positive moments that the graph of life seems to rise continuously, without us even noticing. But this can set us up for a hard fall when things spiral out of our control. Our mental health can take a hit, and it's almost like a thunderstorm sweeping through a garden that has only ever seen sunshine.

Mental health disorders can manifest in various ways, and the symptoms may differ from person to person. Here are some common signs to look out for:

1. Changes in Mood: Persistent sadness, anxiety, or irritability can indicate a mood disorder such as depression or bipolar disorder. Mood swings that are severe or unprovoked are also a key sign.

2. Withdrawal from Social Activities: If someone begins to withdraw from friends, family, or activities they once enjoyed, it might indicate depression, anxiety, or another mental health issue.

3. Changes in Eating or Sleeping Patterns: Significant changes in appetite or sleep—such as sleeping too much, too little, or having disrupted sleep—can be symptoms of several mental health disorders, including depression and anxiety.

4. Difficulty Concentrating: Trouble focusing, remembering, or making decisions can be associated with various mental health issues, including ADHD, depression, and anxiety.

5. Unexplained Physical Symptoms: Sometimes mental health disorders present as physical problems, such as stomach aches, headaches, or other unexplained aches and pains.

6. Increased Sensitivity: Heightened sensitivity to sounds, sights, smells, or touch, or the avoidance of overstimulating situations, may suggest an anxiety disorder or post-traumatic stress disorder (PTSD).

7. Substance Abuse: Using substances like alcohol or drugs to cope with feelings or to avoid them is a common sign of an underlying mental health disorder.

8. Extreme Changes in Behaviour: Any drastic change in behaviour, such as reckless actions or a significant decline in functioning at work or school, could indicate a mental health disorder.

Understanding and Managing Mental Health

Recognising the signs of mental health disorders is just the beginning, and what we've discussed is just the tip of the iceberg. It's equally important to seek help, whether through therapy, medication, or support from loved ones. In India, there is still a significant stigma around mental health, which can make it difficult for people to seek the help they need. However, initiatives like the National Mental Health Programme (NMHP) are working to improve mental health services and raise awareness across the country.

Our mental health is just as important as our physical health. While life might throw unexpected challenges our way, equipping ourselves with the knowledge and tools to maintain our mental health can help us survive those storms. If you're experiencing any of the symptoms mentioned or feel like you're struggling, remember that it's okay to seek help. Just as you wouldn't ignore a physical injury, don't ignore your mental health. It's time to start treating our mental wellbeing as the essential part of our lives that it truly is.

Personally, my mental recovery and overall wellbeing were built on three essential pillars: social, emotional, and financial stability.

The Social Pillar

During the most challenging times, I realised that I couldn't do it all alone. Losing my sister and watching my father's health decline left me feeling isolated and emotionally drained. It was during this period that I truly understood the importance of having a strong social network.

Maintaining regular contact with family and friends became my lifeline. I made it a point to reach out, even if just to say a quick hello or share a laugh. Technology was a godsend here; video calls and group chats became my way of staying connected when physical meetings weren't possible. I can't emphasise enough how much this helped me. It wasn't just about having people to talk to; it was about feeling connected and supported. My friends became a sounding board, helping me to see things from different perspectives and, more importantly, bringing lightness and humour into my life when I needed it most.

One of the best decisions I made was to join the Rotary Club of Bombay Bayview. Initially, I thought of it as a distraction, a way to keep busy and avoid sinking into my thoughts. But it turned into something I absolutely cherish. Engaging with like-minded individuals who were involved in community service and various projects provided me with a renewed sense of purpose and inspiration. It was more than just socialising; it was about being part of something bigger, which helped me find meaning during a time when I felt lost.

The Emotional Pillar

Understanding and managing my emotions was another crucial aspect of my recovery. For a long time, I thought I had to carry the weight of my feelings alone, which only made things worse. It wasn't until I started journaling that I found a way to organise my thoughts and emotions.

At first, I was sceptical about journaling – it seemed like just another buzzword. But I gave it a shot, and it turned out to be incredibly liberating. Journaling allowed me to compartmentalise my feelings about work, family, and personal challenges. It gave me a structured way to approach my daily life, which was especially helpful when everything felt chaotic. Writing down my thoughts made them more manageable, and over time, I noticed a significant improvement in how I handled stress and emotions.

However, journaling alone wasn't enough. There were issues I couldn't discuss with anyone—not my friends, not my family—and that's where therapy came in. Seeking professional help was a game-changer for me. It wasn't just about talking to someone; it was about learning tools and strategies to manage my emotions more effectively. Techniques like Eye Movement Desensitisation and Reprocessing (EMDR) were particularly helpful in dealing with trauma and emotional distress. Therapy gave me the space to process my grief and find ways to move forward.

The Financial Pillar

Financial stability might not seem directly related to mental health, but trust me, it's a huge factor. When I lost my father, I also lost the financial security he provided. Suddenly, I was thrust into a position where I had to take control of my finances, and it was overwhelming.

Thankfully, my brother and son were incredibly proactive in helping me out. They guided me through the basics of financial management—budgeting, saving, and investing. But more than that, they provided the emotional support I needed to make those tough decisions. I learned the importance of creating a financial plan with both short-term and long-term goals. It wasn't just about securing my financial future; it was about regaining a sense of control and stability in my life. Knowing that I had a plan in place allowed me to focus more on my emotional and social wellbeing without constantly worrying about money.

Bringing It All Together

Addressing these three pillars—social, emotional, and financial—wasn't just about tackling different aspects of my life; it was about understanding that they are interconnected and collectively contribute to my overall mental health. By fortifying these areas, I was able to build a foundation that helped me weather the storms that came my way.

This journey taught me that mental health is multifaceted. While these exact pillars may not be the ones affecting your life, tackling your mental health requires a holistic approach, one that considers the full spectrum of our lives. The challenges I faced were tough, but by focusing on these pillars, I found a way to not only survive but thrive. And if you're going through something similar, I hope my experience can provide some insight into how you might start your own journey toward better mental health.

Vision Boards

A vision board is a powerful tool that can help you visualise your goals and dreams. My coveted vision board hangs above my study table in my room, where I can see it all the time. By creating a tangible representation of your aspirations, you can maintain focus and motivation. This task is not only fun to do every couple of months, it is also extremely gratifying to see things on your vision board coming to life.

Start by reflecting on various areas of your life, such as career, health, relationships, and personal growth. What do you want to achieve in these domains? Be specific about your goals to make them more attainable. They don't have to be your end goals in life, but more like achievable milestones that would make you proud.

After this, look for images, quotes, and words that resonate with your goals. These can come from magazines, online sources, or even your own drawings. The key is to choose visuals that inspire you and reflect your aspirations. I find Pinterest to be a great source for this step.

Arrange your images and words on a board or a digital platform. Make sure it's visually appealing and easy to look at. Place your vision board somewhere you'll see it regularly, like your bedroom or workspace, to keep your goals at the forefront of your mind.

Creating a vision board is not just a creative exercise; it's a motivational tool that can keep you focused on your goals. It serves as a constant reminder of what you're working towards, helping you stay committed and driven.

Journaling

Journaling is a therapeutic practice that can significantly enhance your mental health. It allows you to express your thoughts and feelings, track your progress, and reflect on your experiences. I am aware that I am someone who feels low in the evenings, so I always schedule journaling time for that time.

Writing about your experiences can reduce stress and help you process emotions. It provides an outlet for your feelings, which can prevent them from building up and becoming overwhelming. If you are going through a rough phase with someone at work, for example, you can write down objectively how and why that is happening. This will not only help you view the problem from an external lens, but you might just come up with the solution to the problem itself!

Journaling can lead to insights about yourself and your patterns of thinking and behaviour. It can help you identify triggers for certain emotions and understand how to manage them better. A lot of the time, I carry my journal to my therapy sessions to help my therapist understand me better because I may not be feeling the same extent of my emotions during my session, but they might still need to be conveyed.

Use your journal to set and track goals. Reflecting on your progress can keep you motivated and focused. You can also use your journal to brainstorm solutions to challenges you face. These goals can be as small as daily water intake, to larger things like working out three times a week, or completing a big, stressful project.

To start journaling, make sure to find a quiet space where you can write without distractions; the last thing you want is to be distracted by your problem while writing about it. Begin by writing about your day, your thoughts, and your feelings. Don't worry about grammar or structure; the goal is to express yourself freely. Over time, you'll develop a habit of journaling that can bring clarity and calm to your mind. Plus, even within journaling, there are several different techniques that you can employ, like bullet journaling and timeboxing.

Seeking Professional Help

I know I might sound like a broken record, but seeking professional help is a crucial step in managing mental health. Therapists and counsellors can provide valuable support and guidance, offering strategies for coping with stress, managing emotions, and improving mental health. Here's how to find the right therapist and what to expect:

1. Research: Look for licensed professionals with experience in the areas you need help with. You can ask for recommendations from friends, family, or your primary care doctor. Online directories and mental health organisations also provide lists of qualified therapists.

2. Compatibility: It's essential to find a therapist you feel comfortable with. The therapeutic relationship is based on trust and openness, so don't hesitate to switch therapists if the first one isn't the right fit.

3. Commitment: Regular sessions and active participation are crucial for the effectiveness of therapy. Be open and honest with your therapist about your thoughts and feelings, and be willing to try the strategies they suggest.

Professional help can provide a structured and supportive environment to work through your mental health challenges. Therapy can offer new perspectives and coping mechanisms, helping you cope with difficult times more effectively.

Exercise and Physical Health

You'd be surprised how connected physical health and mental health really are. Regular exercise can boost your mood, reduce stress, and improve overall wellbeing. Choose exercises that you find enjoyable, whether it's dancing, hiking, swimming, or yoga. The more you enjoy the activity, the more likely you are to stick with it. If going to the gym four times a week seems intimidating to you, you don't have to do it. Find your own special activity. That way, you will be able to start with small, achievable goals and gradually increase the intensity and duration of your workouts. This approach prevents burnout and keeps you motivated.

Just remember to aim for regular physical activity, even if it's just a short walk each day. Consistency is more important than intensity. Over time, regular exercise can lead to significant improvements in your mental and physical health. Exercise releases endorphins, which are chemicals in the brain that act as natural painkillers and mood elevators. It also helps reduce levels of the body's stress hormones, such as adrenaline and cortisol. Regular physical activity can lead to better sleep, increased energy levels, and improved overall health, contributing to a positive mental state.

Digital Health

In today's digital age, our online interactions and the way we use technology can have a significant impact on our mental health. Don't you feel a weird pang when you see someone fitter, happier, or richer than you on social media? I know I've been there, and it isn't pleasant. But that's the reality of life; neither can we avoid it completely, nor are we built to be okay about them.

By being intentional about your digital habits, you can create a healthier relationship with technology that supports your mental health rather than detracts from it. Curate the content you consume, and above all, remember to know when to detox.

Overcoming the Stigma of Mental Health

Mental health stigma can prevent people from seeking the help they need. It's essential to challenge and overcome this stigma to create a supportive environment for mental health. When I was at my lowest, I didn't even consider seeking help until my kids spoke sense into me. That's because internally I still felt that unspoken judgement. After my kids spoke to me, I went on the internet and tried to educate myself. Understanding the realities of mental health issues really helped reduce my fear and judgement.

You need to talk openly about your mental health with friends, family, and colleagues. Sharing your experiences can encourage others to seek help and foster a more supportive community, and it can even give them a subtle cue on what things trigger you.

Overcoming stigma is crucial for creating an environment where people feel safe and supported in seeking help for their mental health. By fostering open conversations and supporting mental health initiatives, we can work towards a more understanding and compassionate society.

Mental health is a journey, not a destination. It requires ongoing effort, self-compassion, and support from others. By understanding the importance of mental health, embracing solitude, and nurturing the three pillars of social, emotional, and financial wellbeing, you can build a resilient and optimistic mindset. Remember, it's okay to seek help and take steps towards improving your mental health. You are not alone in this journey. Keep moving forward, and know that every step you take is a step towards a brighter future.

Key Learnings

1. Mental health is not just about mood; it encompasses emotional, psychological, and social wellbeing. It affects how we think, feel, act, manage stress, relate to others, and make decisions.

2. Mental health problems are widespread, with the World Health Organisation estimating that one in four people will be affected at some point in their lives. This highlights the importance of recognising signs and seeking help.

3. Three Pillars of Mental Health:
   a. Social Pillar: Maintaining strong social connections provides emotional support, reduces stress, and fosters a sense of belonging.
   b. Emotional Pillar: Understanding and managing emotions through self-awareness, self-compassion, and emotional regulation is crucial.
   c. Financial Pillar: Financial stability reduces stress and anxiety, contributing to overall mental wellbeing.

4. Addressing and overcoming the stigma surrounding mental health is essential for creating a supportive environment where people feel safe to seek help and understand you better.

Action Items

1. Dedicate time each day to write about your thoughts, feelings, and experiences. Use your journal to set and track personal goals and reflect on your progress. It might be helpful to schedule this during a time when you know you won't be feeling great mentally so that you can fill that void by doing something productive.

2. Identify specific goals in different areas of your life. Collect images, quotes, and words that resonate with these goals and arrange them on a board where you can see them regularly.

3. Take steps to improve your financial management skills. Create a budget, set financial goals, and seek advice from knowledgeable individuals or online courses to gain control over your finances. A strong financial situation positively influences your emotional and social decisions, enabling greater stability and confidence.

4. Find an exercise routine you enjoy and can commit to consistently, whether it's a daily walk, yoga, dancing, or any other form of physical activity.

Chapter 12

LEVERAGE YOUR PRIVILEGE

Life is a journey filled with opportunities to discover and become your true self. However, no matter what you achieve in your long journey of learning and unlearning, the essence of a fulfilling life lies not in accolades or titles, but in the impact you have and the lives you touch on your way. We had discussed the importance of peeling back the layers of yourself in the first chapter, and I think it's only pertinent to circle back to that in the last chapter because it all boils down to that. Life is just a big journey of introspection and self-awareness; the better you get at that skill, the easier it'll be to improve your own life while impacting that of others positively.

Everyone has a certain set of strengths that make them unique. These are the qualities and skills that come most naturally to you and set you apart. Using them to your advantage in both personal and professional spheres will not only keep you content in yourself but also help you assist those people who lack in those qualities.

For me, this journey started with identifying what truly mattered to me. I realised that my values of integrity, compassion, and creativity would guide my actions and decisions. I pursued activities that brought me joy and fulfilment, such as travelling, learning, and meeting new people. These experiences not only enriched my life but also helped me understand my unique strengths. Embracing these strengths allowed me to persevere through both personal and professional challenges with confidence and authenticity.

Living a Meaningful Life
Living a life of meaning involves far more than just personal gratification, and I am not talking about doing

something great that impacts the whole world and ends up making you famous. It's more about contributing to something greater than yourself; making a difference in the lives of others, even if it's just a select few. Authenticity is the cornerstone of my life. Being true to myself, even when it is difficult, fosters genuine connections and allows me to live without regrets; an added bonus to this is that I automatically attract other people with the urge to value authenticity; making friends along the way is so easy when you can be unabashedly yourself.

Serving others brings a profound sense of purpose and contentment. Whether volunteering at a local shelter or mentoring someone in need, acts of kindness and service always make a significant difference. Creating positive change has become a mission, and I try to use my skills and resources to advocate for causes I believe in. This even sowed the seed for me to start my own initiative someday, a place where the youth could learn through my experience and skillset.

Reflecting on personal experiences provides powerful insights into the journey of becoming your true self and leaving a legacy. Overcoming adversity was a significant part of my journey. I faced challenges, including the loss of loved ones and personal setbacks, which taught me resilience and the importance of sound mental health. Sharing these stories, I hope to inspire others to persevere and find strength in difficult times. Empowering the youth is my utmost passion. I have dedicated my life to mentoring and guiding young individuals. Through workshops, public speaking, and personal interactions, I have witnessed firsthand the transformative power of confidence-building and skill development.

If I didn't strive to keep learning continuously, I wouldn't be able to achieve even half of what I'm proud of today. I committed to educating myself, staying abreast of new developments, and honing my skills. I didn't need to go out of the way, spend money and time, and do courses from institutions around the world, but I knew how this would affect the broader picture. This enabled me to adapt and thrive in any dynamic environment with agility. Creating a lasting impact involves developing actionable steps that align with who you are. Focus on improving your skills and expanding your knowledge. This not only enhances your capabilities but also equips you to contribute more effectively.

Building a network of like-minded individuals who share your vision and values amplifies your impact. Engage in community initiatives and contribute to local causes. These efforts foster a sense of belonging and allow you to make a tangible difference in your immediate environment. Besides this, mentoring and teaching are essential aspects of leaving a legacy. One must always share their expertise and experiences. You don't have to be in your fifties with years of experience to do this; suppose, if you're great at math, you could take time to help out your peers who aren't, and don't shy away from learning something from them that they might be good at. This helps build a channel of knowledge and empowerment, ensuring that your impact continues long after you're gone.

In all honesty, I didn't have that. I had to learn many lessons the hard way. There were times when others held my hand, but only momentarily. My strongest suits are those I had to inculcate by myself. Sometimes, self-reliance is a testament to the importance of continuous growth and adaptation. I have become a point of contact for the youth. Young people message me about their issues, whether it's about dressing, reading, or building confidence. It's a role I cherish, knowing that my guidance helps them in some way. I love the concept of "train the trainer." You cannot teach how to swim online; it needs to happen one-on-one. My passion for power skills and energising the youth confidently cannot be achieved alone. I want to create multiple champions, individuals who play the same role as I do – helping, guiding, mentoring, and nurturing. When you impart your knowledge, you are essentially creating many different versions of yourself. These versions will carry forward this knowledge to a much larger audience, and it will all trace back to YOU.

Leaving a legacy isn't something you consciously strive for; it's the natural outcome of living with purpose and passion. When you focus on what truly matters and pursue it wholeheartedly, you create an impact that lasts far beyond your presence. Whether through social media or in personal interactions, I've always believed that living authentically and giving selflessly paves the way for a legacy worth remembering. Leverage your privileges to uplift others, and in doing so, you'll leave behind something far greater than material success – a life that inspires.

Addressing Modern Challenges

Social media has become an integral part of our lives, providing a platform for connection, learning, and entertainment. However, the addictive nature of these platforms poses a significant challenge. While I am not against social media, I am deeply concerned about the addiction that comes with it. People of all ages are affected, often spending hours scrolling through feeds, which can lead to decreased productivity and increased anxiety.

Deleting the app is not a solution. Instead, we need to understand why social media is taking over our lives and find ways to manage our time better. Implementing time management strategies can help. For instance, setting specific times of the day for social media use, using app limits, and prioritising tasks can significantly reduce the time spent on these platforms. By planning your day well and focusing on your priorities, social media can become a reward rather than a distraction.

Achieving a balance between work and personal life is another significant challenge. The demands of work, coupled with personal responsibilities, can lead to burnout and a sense of unfulfillment. It's essential to set boundaries and prioritise self-care to maintain a healthy balance.

One effective strategy is to create a clear distinction between work and personal time. Establishing a routine that includes time for relaxation, hobbies, and social activities can help prevent burnout. It's also important to communicate your boundaries with colleagues and family members to ensure that your personal time is respected.

Embracing Your Journey

As we conclude this book, I encourage you to take the lessons and insights shared and apply them to your life. Strive to become your true self, live a life of meaning, and leave a legacy that reflects your values and passions. Remember, the journey is just as important as the destination. Keep moving forward, and know that every step you take is a step towards a brighter and more impactful future.

Reflect on what you want to be remembered for. For me, it's not about being the most innovative or enterprising. I want to be remembered as a happy, fun person who handled life with grace, embraced a growth mindset, and found happiness within myself. I aspire to be someone who creates a beautiful life through traveling, learning, and meeting new people.

Most importantly, I want to impact the youth. I aspire to guide generations in building their confidence, whether in professional or personal spheres. I dream of owning a school that uses all my guidance, power, and personal touch – a place where the youth will remember me as 'AB Inspires'.

Creating modules for skill development, certification courses on speaking, dressing, and power skills – these are part of the change I aim to bring. I want to give millennials and gen Z the confidence to overcome anxiety and face the world with strength and resilience.

As we reach the end of this journey together, it is essential to remember the importance of leveraging our privilege. Privilege, in its many forms, is not just a ticket to personal gain but a profound responsibility. Whether it's the privilege of education, financial stability, a supportive network, or even just the power of a healthy mind and body, these are assets that must be used not only for our own growth but to uplift others. The real measure of our success isn't found in what we accumulate but in what we give back, in the bridges we build, and in the lives we touch. As we chisel out our own paths, let's commit to using our strengths and resources to create positive ripples in the world around us. By consciously choosing to share, support, and empower, we turn our privilege into purpose, ensuring that our impact extends far beyond ourselves, shaping a future that is brighter, more inclusive, and full of hope for everyone. Let this be our lasting legacy—where our privilege creates champions who are compassionate, connected, and confident, changing lives.

Key Learnings

1. True fulfilment lies in impact. Achievements and accolades are important, but the true essence of a fulfilling life is found in the impact you have on others and the legacy you leave behind.
2. Modern challenges like social media addiction, procrastination, and information overload can impede personal growth and productivity. Managing these effectively through time management, setting boundaries, and continuous learning is crucial.
3. Lifelong learning and staying updated with new developments are essential for personal and professional growth. Embracing change and adapting to new situations help in remaining relevant and impactful.
4. Mentoring and guiding the youth, sharing experiences, and building confidence in them are vital for creating a lasting legacy.

Action Items

1. Create a daily schedule that includes specific times for social media use, work, relaxation, and hobbies. Use tools like app limits and timers to manage time effectively.
2. Distinguish between work and personal time. Communicate these boundaries to colleagues and family members to ensure a healthy work-life balance. Include regular breaks and leisure activities in your routine to prevent burnout.

3. Share your knowledge and experiences with others, especially the youth. Volunteer for mentorship programmes and provide guidance on personal and professional growth based on your own learnings. Establish a network of like-minded individuals to amplify your impact.

ABOUT THE AUTHOR

Arwa Baldiwala's journey has been anything but conventional. Struggling with self-doubt and a crippling fear of public speaking in her early years, she often questioned her ability to make an impact. However, it was this very struggle that ignited her passion to uplift and empower others.

Today, with over 22 years of impactful experience in education, Arwa is a visionary leader and a staunch advocate for fostering resilience and self-assurance in Millennials and Gen Z. As a lifelong learner with a growth mindset, she recently completed the prestigious School Turnaround Leaders Program at the Harvard Graduate School of Education (Massachusetts), a testament to her commitment to excellence.

Additionally, as an accredited International Coaching Federation (ICF) Youth Advisor and the driving force behind the transformative Power Skills Program, she equips young adults with essential tools to thrive in a chaotic, ever-evolving world.

Her debut book, *Double Tap on Life*, is a heartfelt guide that draws from her personal journey and professional expertise. Through its pages, Arwa offers actionable insights to help readers overcome self-doubt, embrace growth, and unlock their full potential. This book is her way of paying it forward—a roadmap to empower others to create confident, fulfilling lives.

She can be reached at:
LinkedIn – www.linkedin.com/in/arwabaldiwala
Instagram – arwa.baldiwala
Website – arwabaldiwala.com